LOCOMOTION PAPERS  LP226

The Wrexham & Ellesmere Railway

by
Stanley C. Jenkins & John M. Strange

THE OAKWOOD PRESS

© Oakwood Press 2004

British Library Cataloguing in Publication Data
A Record for this book is available from the British Library
ISBN 0 85361 617 5

Typeset by Oakwood Graphics.
Repro by Ford Graphics, Ringwood, Hants.
Printed by Cambrian Printers Ltd, Aberystwyth, Ceredigion

All rights reserved. No part of this book may be reproduced or transmitted in any form or by any means, electronic or mechanical, including photocopying, recording or by any information storage and retrieval system, without permission from the Publisher in writing.

Note on Station and Viaduct Names

Bangor and Overton stations were both regarded as being 'on Dee' to differentiate them from Bangor on the LNWR North Wales line and Overton on the LSWR main line (between Basingstoke and Andover). The names chosen for the halts were, in most cases, somewhat less precise. Whereas Hightown and Trench halts obviously took their names from nearby places that would have been recognised by the average traveller, some of the other stopping places appear to have been named after neighbouring country houses such as Pickhill Hall and Cloy Hall; although opened in 1932 as 'Caedyah Halt', 'Cloy Halt' was soon adopted as the name of the the latter stopping place.

There is considerable confusion in terms of the names applied to the viaducts on the Wrexham & Ellesmere line, the official GWR nomenclature being, in most cases, at variance with local names. The Willow Road viaduct, for instance, is more often known as the Tuttle Street bridge while the Kings Mill viaduct is sometimes known as the Clywedog viaduct.

The Kings Mill Siding, serving the Kingsmill Brick Works, is in the hamlet of King's Mills which, to a Welsh speaker, might also be known as Pentre'r Felin Newydd! (Felin, of course, being Welsh for mill.)

Title page: Collett 0-4-2T No. 1432 awaits departure from Wrexham Central with the 1.30 pm to Ellesmere on 1st May, 1962 The driver (*nearest the camera*) was V. Aldridge of Oswestry shed.
John White

Front cover: Collett '14XX' class 0-4-2T No. 1458 with the branch passenger service at Overton-on-Dee in April 1962.
John M. Strange

Rear cover, top: Ellesmere station, with the auto-train for Wrexham standing in the down platform.
John M. Strange

Rear cover, bottom: The auto-train awaits departure from Wrexham in April 1962.
John M. Strange

Published by The Oakwood Press (Usk), P.O. Box 13, Usk, Mon., NP15 1YS.
E-mail: oakwood-press@dial.pipex.com
Website: www.oakwood-press.dial.pipex.com

Contents

	John Strange (1936-2003)	4
	Introduction	5
	Historical Summary	7
Chapter One	**Origins of the Wrexham & Ellesmere Branch**	
	The Formation of the Cambrian Railways - The Whitchurch, Wrexham, Mold & Connah's Quay Junction Railway - Influence of the Manchester, Sheffield & Lincolnshire Railway - Formation of the Wrexham & Ellesmere Railway - An Agreement with the Great Western? - Directors & Promoters: A Further Note	9
Chapter Two	**Construction and Opening of the Wrexham & Ellesmere Railway**	
	Boardroom Changes - Construction Begins - The First Passenger-Carrying Train - Completion & Opening of the Wrexham Railway - Some Details of the Line	19
Chapter Three	**Developments during the Cambrian and Great Western Periods**	
	Locomotives and Train Services in the Early 20th Century - World War I and the Grouping - Changes and Improvements during the Great Western Period - Operating the Line during the Great Western Era Collection & Delivery Arrangements - Goods Trains and Traffic - World War II	37
Chapter Four	**The Stations and Route from Ellesmere to Sesswick**	
	Ellesmere - Ellesmere 'Old Loop Siding' - Elson Halt - Elson Siding - Trench Halt and Siding - Overton-on-Dee - Cloy Halt - Bangor-on-Dee - Pickhill Halt and Cadbury's Siding - Sesswick Halt	65
Chapter Five	**The Stations and Route from Sesswick to Wrexham**	
	Marchwiel Royal Ordnance Factory Sidings - Marchwiel - Five Fords Farm Siding - Abenbury Brick Works Siding - Kings Mill Brick Works Siding - Hightown Siding and Halt - Wrexham (Caia) Goods Yard - Wrexham Central - A Note on Distances	95
Chapter Six	**The Final Years 1948-1982**	
	Motive Power in the BR Period - Post-War Rolling Stock - Train Services in the BR Period - Towards Closure - The Last Trains - A Freight-Only Branch - Post-Closure Developments - The Railway Today	119
Appendix One	Chronology	139
Appendix Two	Facilities at Halts and Stations	141
	A Guide to Further Study	143
	Index	144

John Strange (1936-2003)

John Strange spent his childhood on the family farm at St Martin's, near Gobowen in Shropshire, but having rejected a career in farming he decided to become a schoolmaster. He obtained his teaching certificate at the Culham Church of England Teacher Training College, and subsequently worked as a history teacher in Gloucestershire. In 1971, he took an honours degree at the University of Lancaster, after which he taught history at the Ripley St Thomas Church of England School in that city.

In many ways an eccentric, John had homes in both Lancaster and Gobowen. In the latter part of his life he commuted regularly between Lancashire and Shropshire, typically spending a week in Lancaster and then travelling south to Gobowen for a similar period of time. This mode of operation enabled him to indulge in a wide range of activities, while keeping a watchful eye on his elderly aunts in Shropshire.

John's many hobbies and interests included local history, industrial archaeology, railways and real ale. He was particularly keen on the Great Western and Cambrian systems, and had travelled over virtually every part of the GWR network, collecting at least one Edmondson card ticket from each station, and photographing many lines and stations that have since been closed. He was also an enthusiastic train-spotter, who had seen all of the GWR 'Castles' and many other famous locomotive classes.

An interest in railway history led, perhaps inevitably, to an interest in canals, and in this context John was a co-owner of the 70 ft narrow boat *Towy* - a former Clayton 'tanker' that has been restored as a sheeted boat and has often been displayed at the Boat Museum, Ellesmere Port.

The Campaign for Real Ale (CAMRA) was another of John's interests. He was an active member of his local CAMRA branches, and would travel many miles to visit particular pubs or sample famous 'brews'. He recorded large numbers of pubs and local breweries, many of which have subsequently closed - numerous inns or pubs being photographed to provide information on inn signs, liveries or other details. Pub visits would often be combined with canal trips or railway journeys, these aspects of local history being a 'seamless garment' in John's eyes.

In 2001 John realised that he was seriously ill, but he insisted that his condition was not terminal and, having refused medical treatment, he attempted to maintain his very full lifestyle. He collapsed in his local pub, the Cross Foxes at Gobowen, on 23rd December, 2003 and was taken to the Maelor Hospital, Wrexham, where he died on Christmas Day 2003. His death was a great shock to his many friends and acquaintances, none of whom had known that he was mortally ill. John's ashes are interred in the family grave at St Martin's - the Shropshire village in which he had lived as a child and young man.   *Stanley C. Jenkins*

Right: John Strange points out the site of Blodwell Junction on the Tanat Valley Railway.

Introduction

In 1922 the Great Western Railway (GWR) absorbed or amalgamated with a number of hitherto independent Welsh railways. The largest company involved in this comprehensive 'Grouping' scheme was the Cambrian Railways Company, which operated a long, straggling main line from Whitchurch in the east to Aberystwyth and Pwllheli in the west. The Cambrian system also encompassed several branch lines, one of which was the nominally-independent Wrexham & Ellesmere Railway.

The Wrexham & Ellesmere line could trace its beginnings back to the 1860s when, during a period of feverish speculation that has sometimes been called 'the second Railway Mania', the Wrexham, Mold & Connah's Quay Railway (WM&CQ) had attempted to complete a rail link between Wrexham and Whitchurch. Although initially unsuccessful, the original scheme eventually found tangible form as the Wrexham & Ellesmere Railway, which was promoted some 20 years later. The line was opened in 1895, and it then formed an end-on junction with the Wrexham, Mold & Connah's Quay Railway; the new line was worked by the Cambrian Railways and, for a few years at least, this single track branch formed part of a tenuous cross-country link between Manchester and Liverpool and the districts served by the Cambrian system.

In the longer term, the Wrexham & Ellesmere line failed to develop into an important main line because it was in direct competition with the much larger GWR system for traffic to and from South and Central Wales. Moreover, the 1922-1923 Grouping ensured that the line passed into Great Western hands, whereas the Wrexham, Mold & Connah's Quay route became part of the newly-created London & North Eastern Railway (LNER). Thereafter, both of these border lines became little more than local branch lines - though intrepid through travellers were still able to travel northwards beyond Wrexham if they changed from the trains of one company to another at Wrexham Central station.

The Great Western treated the Wrexham & Ellesmere route as an ordinary country branch line, and in the 1920s and 1930s this 12½ mile single track route would have been very similar to scores of other rural lines throughout the far-reaching GWR network. In World War II the route carried extra traffic to and from a large ordnance factory that had been established at Marchwiel, and in post-war years the site of this factory became an industrial estate that continued to provide freight traffic for the railway.

Sadly, the Wrexham & Ellesmere line did not survive the anti-railway purges of the 1960s, and its passenger services were withdrawn in 1962. Freight traffic continued to operate over the northern end of the line until the 1980s, but complete closure finally came in 1981.

The Wrexham & Ellesmere line is of interest for several reasons; it was a true 'border' branch, being partly in England and partly in Wales, while its independent status - albeit nominal - lasted until the Grouping. For modellers, the line could boast three small, but attractive country stations, together with six smaller Halts and several private goods sidings. The two stations at each end of the route were also of considerable interest - Ellesmere being a relatively compact country junction while Wrexham was an unusual example of a 'through terminus', one side being used by the Cambrian/GWR whereas the other half of the station was served by terminating Great Central/LNER traffic.

Passengers disembark at Elson Halt in April 1961. The locomotive is Collett '14XX' class 0-4-2T No. 1438.
John M. Strange

No. 1458 at Wrexham Central on 19th May, 1962. Note the Cambrian Railways trespass sign.

INTRODUCTION

There has not, hitherto, been a history of the line, and very few articles have been written; neither has the route received much attention from casual photographers. This present volume therefore fills a small but significant gap in the railway history of the Welsh border region, and it is hoped that the details will be of interest to modellers and local historians, as well as railway enthusiasts and other readers.

A generally chronological framework has been followed, *Chapter One* being devoted to the early history of the scheme, while *Chapter Two* covers the construction, opening and early years of the Wrexham & Ellesmere Railway. *Chapter Three* contains details of locomotives, train services and general development during the period from 1900 until 1947, and the following chapters deal in greater detail with the stations and infrastructure of the line. Finally, *Chapter Six* is devoted to the British Railways (BR) period from 1948 until final closure in 1981.

The book is a joint effort between Stanley Jenkins and John Strange. Stanley Jenkins, a museum curator and professional historian, has provided the text and carried out most of the documentary research, while John Strange, a former history teacher, has concentrated on the search for photographs and other illustrative material. As a native of St Martin's, near Gobowen he has also furnished local detail, and carried out numerous interviews with former GWR and BR staff in the Oswestry area.

Thanks are due to various people for help in the preparation of this study, including John Alsop, Sid Barclay, Stephen Bell, David Castledine of the Denbighshire Record Office, Revd Alan Cliff, Michael Davie, the late C.C. Green, Frank Jones, R.W. Miller, Paul Mottram, David Sallery, the late John Smith, Dave Southern, Ken Southern, Chris Turner, Jack Wilkinson and Martin Williams.

Historical Summary

Company of Origin: Wrexham & Ellesmere Railway, incorporated 31st July, 1885, with powers to construct a railway commencing at Wrexham by a junction with the Wrexham, Mold & Connah's Quay and terminating at Ellesmere by a junction with the Oswestry & Whitchurch line.

Length of Line: Ellesmere station to Wrexham Central station 12 miles 57 chains (Cambrian Junction to Wrexham 12 miles 46 chains).

Typical Motive Power: '14XX' class 0-4-2Ts; '517' class 0-4-2Ts; '74XX' class 0-6-0PTs; '57XX' class 0-6-0PTs; '54XX' class 0-6-0PTs; '81XX' class 2-6-2Ts, class '25' diesel Bo-Bos.

Route Colour: All 'Yellow and 'Uncoloured' locomotives permitted, together with 'Blue' locomotives subject to local restrictions.

Principal Engineering Works: Dee viaduct (66 yds) ; Forge Mill viaduct (34 yards), Kings Mill viaduct (84 yds); Tuttle Hill or Willow Road viaduct (69 yds); Town Hill viaduct (68 yds).

Operation of Line (1944): Single line track between Ellesmere and Wrexham Central (South box) worked by electric train token between Ellesmere and Overton-on-Dee, Overton-on-Dee and Bangor-on-Dee, and Marchwiel Factory and Marchwiel; electric train tablet between Bangor-on-Dee and Marchwiel Factory and Marchwiel and Wrexham Central.

Dates of Closure: Passenger services withdrawn from whole line on Saturday 8th September, 1962. Goods services withdrawn from Ellesmere to Marchwiel (exclusive) in September 1962. Line cut back to Abenbury in 1973, and closed in its entirety in 1981.

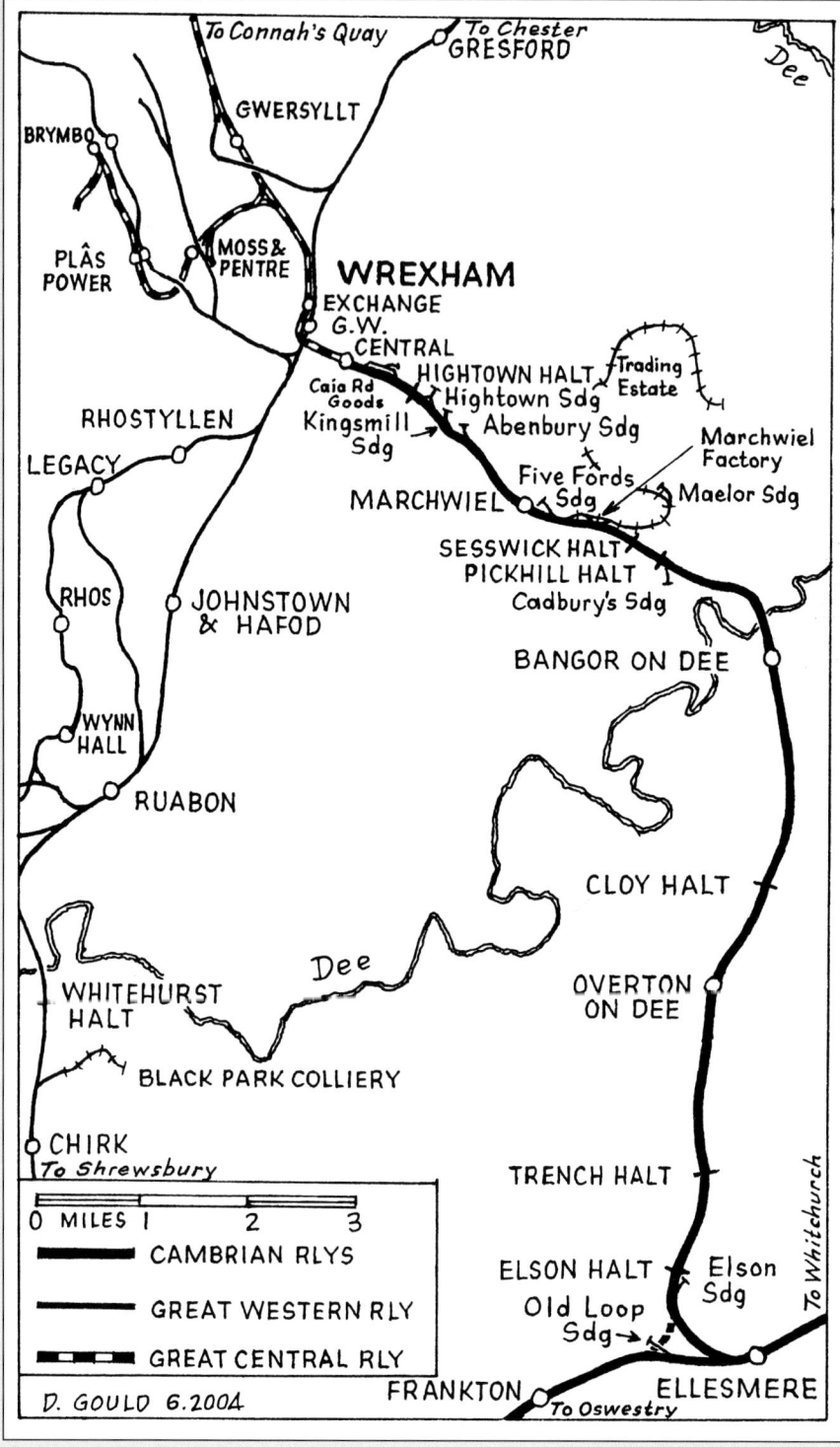

Chapter One

Origins of the Wrexham & Ellesmere Branch

The Cambrian is generally regarded as a purely Welsh line, but in practice it had originated in the Welsh borders, and its Oswestry headquarters was actually in England. Indeed, the company was well-established in Shropshire, and in addition to the main line from Whitchurch to Oswestry, three Cambrian branch lines were situated partly on the English side of the border - these being the Llanfyllin, Tanat Valley and Wrexham lines (all of which started in England and finished in Wales!).

In reality the origins of the Cambrian system are surprisingly complex, the northern part of the Welsh borders having seen much promotional activity during the 19th century as competing railway companies struggled for control of the Welsh coal traffic. One of the first companies in the field was the Shrewsbury, Oswestry & Chester Junction Railway, which soon joined forces with the North Wales Mineral Railway to form the Shrewsbury & Chester Railway. The Shrewsbury & Chester line, which was completed throughout on 14th October, 1848, eventually became part of the GWR system; thereafter, the GWR was reluctant to allow other lines into the area.

In the event, the Great Western was faced with considerable opposition from the London & North Western Railway (LNWR) and other companies, with the result that some of the Welsh border lines were eventually brought under joint GWR/LNWR control. This development did not, however, prevent rival companies from entering the arena, and in this context the Cambrian Railways were formed as a direct challenge to the two big companies.

The Formation of the Cambrian Railways

The Cambrian system originated with the promotion of the Oswestry & Newtown Railway in 1855. This line was opened from Oswestry as far as Pool Quay on 1st May, 1860, and extended to Welshpool in August 1860; finally, on 10th June, 1861 the Oswestry & Newtown was completed throughout to Newtown in Montgomeryshire, where connection was made with an existing line to Llanidloes which had been opened for freight traffic on 30th April, 1859 and for passengers on 31st August.

At its northern end, the Oswestry & Newtown Railway formed a connection with the GWR branch from Gobowen, which had been opened under Shrewsbury & Chester auspices on 1st January, 1849. Needless to say, this arrangement ensured that the Oswestry & Newtown Railway and its allies would be dependent on GWR co-operation and goodwill - otherwise, these independent Welsh lines would have no outlet for traffic to and from the populous areas of England.

In the meantime, the Oswestry, Ellesmere & Whitchurch Railway had been formed in 1861 as a means of linking the Oswestry & Newtown Railway and other Welsh lines with the London & North Western Railway at Whitchurch; if this route was successfully completed, it would provide a valuable connection with the LNWR system and break the monopoly of the Great Western Railway at Oswestry. In connection with this scheme, another company known as the Whitchurch, Wrexham, Mold & Connah's Quay Railway had published plans for a line running northwards from the Ellesmere line at Bettisfield.

Before implementing their scheme, the supporters of the Ellesmere line had first to seek Parliamentary consent. A Bill was therefore lodged for consideration in the session of 1861 and, despite Great Western opposition, the project seemed destined for success. The proposed line to Whitchurch was strongly supported in Ellesmere; in December 1860, for example, a 'memorial' had been signed by local ratepayers who were 'in favour of the proposed Oswestry, Ellesmere & Whitchurch Railway' and opposed 'to any Branch or other Line proposed by the Great Western Company to Ellesmere'.

Having successfully passed all stages of the complex Parliamentary process, an Act of Parliament authorising the construction and maintenance of the Oswestry, Ellesmere & Whitchurch Railway received the Royal Assent on 1st August, 1861.

The new Act (24 & 25 Vict. cap. 223) provided consent for a railway commencing at Oswestry in the County of Shropshire by a junction with the Oswestry & Newtown Railway and terminating at Whitchurch by a junction with the London & North Western Railway. The authorised line would be 18 miles long, and to pay for its construction the promoters were authorised to raise the sum of £150,000 in £10 shares, with an additional £50,000 by loan. A period of three years was allowed for the compulsory purchase of land, and five years were allowed for completion of the works.

Perversely, Parliament insisted that the eastern section from Whitchurch to Ellesmere should be built first, the idea being that the Great Western Railway might, in the meantime, decide to proceed with a rival scheme for construction of a line to Ellesmere. In the event of such a line being built the two companies would have to come to an agreement concerning running powers over each section.

Work on the Whitchurch to Ellesmere line officially began in August 1861, the ceremonial 'first sod' being cut in a field near Ellesmere Workhouse. The first incision was made with the aid of a specially decorated spade and barrow, and after the sod cutting had taken place the official party attended a grand banquet at which numerous speeches were made. Despite problems with certain landowners who openly supported a rival GWR scheme for a line to Ellesmere, construction was under way by the beginning of 1862 - the line being laid across Fenn's Moss with the aid of deep drains, rafts of faggots and larch poles.

Having managed to defeat the GWR in Parliament, the Oswestry, Ellesmere & Whitchurch supporters were able to proceed with their modest, but entirely feasible scheme, and the Whitchurch to Ellesmere section was ready for opening by the spring of 1863. The completion of this first portion of the line was marked by the running of a special train on 20th April, 1863, the first passengers being a company of part-time Rifle Volunteers. This inaugural special was hauled by the Oswestry & Newton Railway locomotives *Montgomery* and *Hero*. The new line was opened just a few days later on 4th May, 1863.

The final section, of a little over seven miles, was not yet ready for opening, and Ellesmere remained the terminus of a branch from Whitchurch for just over one year. Meanwhile, while work continued on the Ellesmere to Oswestry line, the shifting sands of company politics were about to change the entire pattern of railway development in mid-Wales. It was decided that the Oswestry, Ellesmere & Whitchurch Railway would be merged with other local companies to form a much larger company with a whole system of lines in Wales and the Welsh borders.

To achieve this aim, the Oswestry & Newtown, Newtown & Machynlleth, Llanidloes & Newtown and Oswestry, Ellesmere & Whitchurch companies were amalgamated to form the aptly-named Cambrian Railways, an Act for this purpose (27 & 28 Vict. cap. 262) being obtained on 25th July, 1864. Just two days later, on 27th July, 1864, the Ellesmere to Oswestry line was opened to traffic, and the newly-created Cambrian Railways company thereby gained a direct link to England, that was entirely independent of the rival GWR.

The Whitchurch, Wrexham, Mold & Connah's Quay Junction Railway

The proposed Whitchurch, Wrexham, Mold & Connah's Quay Junction Railway was not involved in the Cambrian Railways amalgamation scheme, though its promoters remained closely-connected with the Cambrian Railways project. The WM&CQ company was formed towards the end of 1861, when a group of mine owners, landowners and entrepreneurs met at Wrexham to discuss plans for a rail link serving mines and other industries in the Wrexham area.

The suggested Wrexham, Mold & Connah's Quay Railway would extend northwards from Wrexham, and make connections with other mineral lines in the immediate vicinity. At the same time WM&CQ promoters anticipated that their proposed line would also form a useful connection with the London & North Western Railway near Whitchurch.

Plans of the proposed line from Whitchurch to Wrexham and the River Dee were deposited in November 1861. As far as the southern portion of the line is concerned, these show that the route would have run more or less east-south-east from Wrexham, passing through or near Marchwiel and Bangor-on-Dee; from there, the projected line turned south-eastwards and, running through sparsely-populated agricultural countryside, it continued in a more or less straight line to the proposed junction with the Oswestry, Ellesmere & Whitchurch route at Bettisfield.

The Wrexham, Mold & Connah's Quay Bill was submitted to Parliament in time for the 1862 session. Despite strenuous opposition from the Great Western Railway, the scheme was eventually passed in an amended and severely truncated form.

The Wrexham, Mold & Connah's Quay Railway was incorporated by Act of Parliament on 7th August, 1862 (25 & 26 Vict. cap. 221) with powers to construct a line from Wrexham to Buckley, where connection would be made with the existing Buckley Railway; the Buckley line, which had opened for mineral traffic on 7th June, 1862, provided a connection to the wharves at Connah's Quay, from which coal and minerals could be exported by coastal vessels.

To pay for their scheme, the WM&CQ promoters were authorised to raise the sum of £150,000 in £10 shares together with a further £50,000 by loans. A period of three years was allowed for the purchase of land, while five years were allowed for completion of the works. The number of Directors was fixed at nine, the qualification for Board membership being £500. The line was, from its inception, strongly supported by the mine owners and industrialists of the Wrexham and Buckley areas, who realised that improved transport facilities were a vital prerequisite for commercial success.

Unfortunately, the southern part of the WM&CQ scheme between Wrexham and Bettisfield had not survived Parliamentary scrutiny, and the amended Wrexham, Mold & Connah's Quay scheme, as authorised in 1862, consisted of little more than 12 miles of line serving a cluster of coal mines to the north and west of Wrexham.

The Wrexham, Mold & Connah's Quay scheme was still seen, however, as much more than a local mineral line, and its ambitious promoters were keen to extend their authorised route to Whitchurch, Brymbo and elsewhere. In this respect the suggested southern extension from Wrexham to Whitchurch was seen as a particularly important project, as it would enable the WM&CQ company to break out of territory that had hitherto been dominated by the GWR.

Although, as first proposed, the Whitchurch extension line would have formed a junction with the Oswestry, Ellesmere & Whitchurch line at Bettisfield, the WM&CQ promoters soon decided that a direct link to the London & North Western line at Whitchurch would be preferable, and in the Autumn of 1862 a Bill for this and other ambitious extensions was prepared for submission to Parliament.

The new proposals were similar to the original 1861 Whitchurch scheme, but, instead of running south-east towards Bettisfield the amended route proceeded roughly east-south-eastwards via Tallarn Green and Higher Wych, the junction with the LNWR being effected to the north of Whitchurch station. The proposed route would be about 15 miles long, and its steepest gradient was said to be 1 in 80; the estimated cost was £144,076.

In the event, the WM&CQ Directors failed to gain Parliamentary consent for their 1863 extension Bill. A substantially-similar Bill was, in consequence, prepared for submission to Parliament in the 1864 session, the necessary plans and sections being deposited in the previous November.

The 1864 Bill contained a variety of other proposals in addition to the Whitchurch extension scheme, but most of these were deleted; however, on this occasion the Whitchurch extension proposal was received favourably by Parliament, and having passed safely through all stages of the complex Parliamentary process the WM&CQ Extension Bill received the Royal Assent on 25th July, 1864. By this Act (27 & 28 Vict. cap. 234) the Wrexham, Mold & Connah's Quay Railway was empowered to construct extensions to Whitchurch and Brymbo; five years were allowed for completion of the works, and the company was authorised to raise a further £200,000 in shares and £66,600 by loan.

On 29th June, 1865 the WM&CQ company obtained a further Act for construction of a line running north-westwards from the authorised route of the

Whitchurch line at Wrexham to Farndon, in the Dee Valley. Throughout this time, however, the Wrexham, Mold & Connah's Quay Railway remained chronically short of money, and with its original line as yet unfinished, it appeared unlikely that these diverse extension lines would ever get off the ground.

In 1866 the WM&CQ secured another Act, which, among other things, permitted a deviation of the authorised line from Wrexham to Whitchurch. There was, by this time, at least some attempt to begin construction of the extension line in the vicinity of Wrexham, about half a mile of cuttings and embankments being commenced between Hightown and Kings Mills. Meanwhile, on 1st May, 1866, the WM&CQ main line was opened for public traffic between Wrexham and Buckley, a distance of 12½ miles.

An extension of time for completion of the Wrexham to Whitchurch extension was obtained in 1867, but the line was never completed. The WM&CQ Company had been severely hit by the banking crisis that followed the failure of bankers Overend, Gurney & Co. in May 1866, and in these melancholy circumstances it became increasingly difficult for struggling railway companies to raise their authorised capital. By the 1870s all thoughts of extension towards Whitchurch had been abandoned, and the Wrexham, Mold & Connah's Quay Railway settled down to eke out a somewhat impecunious existence as a purely local passenger and mineral-carrying line.

The Influence of the Manchester, Sheffield & Lincolnshire Railway

In later years, the Manchester, Sheffield & Lincolnshire Railway (MS&L) began to take an interest in the WM&CQ line, and with MS&L support this Welsh border line began once more to consider extensions of various kinds, particularly at the northern end, where connection was eventually made with the Manchester, Sheffield & Lincolnshire Railway via the Cheshire Lines system.

The Manchester, Sheffield & Lincolnshire Railway had originated as a northern line, its original heartland being in the Pennine areas of Lancashire and Yorkshire. At the end of the 19th century, however, the MS&L company became more ambitious, and under its energetic Chairman Sir Edward Watkin (1819-1901) the Manchester, Sheffield & Lincolnshire system began to expand in various directions, one obvious source of traffic being the South Wales coal fields. South Wales was, in general, dominated by the GWR, but the presence of the Cambrian Railways offered a way of circumventing the Great Western monopoly.

Although the Cambrian system did not approach anywhere near the original MS&L system, the Cheshire Lines Committee, with its links to Chester and the Welsh borders, formed a suitable route for South Wales coal traffic. With the Wrexham, Mold & Connah's Quay line more or less under MS&L control, it became possible for Manchester, Sheffield & Lincolnshire services to reach as far south as Wrexham, from where it was but a short distance of about 12 miles to Ellesmere on the Cambrian Railways line between Whitchurch and Oswestry.

For this reason the MS&L Railway became intensely interested in the possibility of an extension southwards from Wrexham to Ellesmere, and thus, in the early 1880s, the earlier scheme for a line from Wrexham to the Oswestry, Ellesmere & Whitchurch line was revived. As well as enjoying full MS&L support, the new proposals were welcomed by local residents and businessmen, many of whom were unhappy with the existing GWR services in the Wrexham area.

In 1882 William Davies, the Wrexham, Mold & Connah's Quay Railway Engineer, began surveying a possible route between Wrexham and Welshampton, and in 1884 a Bill for the construction of a proposed 'Denbighshire & Shropshire Union Railway' was submitted to Parliament. This new scheme was, in effect, a revival of the original WM&CQ Bettisfield project, and its principal supporter was Benjamin Piercy - an ambitious promoter of Welsh border railways, and an important figure in the affairs of the Wrexham, Mold & Connah's Quay Railway.

Benjamin Piercy (1828-1888), the son of a Welsh surveyor, had started his railway career as an engineer, but there can be little doubt that he had also made his fortune as a promoter and speculator. By 1884 he was living in considerable style at Marchwiel Hall, near the route of the proposed railway, and it seems likely that he hoped to develop the surrounding area as a mining and industrial district. In this context it may be significant that, in 1870, it had been estimated that the coal seams that were thought to exist in the area contained up to two thousand, five hundred million tons of coal!

The Denbighshire & Shropshire Union Railway Bill was passed by the House of Commons, but problems then arose when the traders and residents of Ellesmere objected to the suggested route of the line, which would have continued south-south-eastwards from Bangor-on-Dee towards Penley, and thence to its junction with the Whitchurch to Oswestry line in the vicinity of Bettisfield. Such a line would have been ideal from an engineering viewpoint, but it had the disadvantage of omitting Ellesmere, and for this reason the Bill was withdrawn pending a reappraisal of the proposed route south of Bangor-on-Dee.

Formation of the Wrexham & Ellesmere Railway

Undeterred by this minor setback, Benjamin Piercy immediately proposed a revised scheme known as The Wrexham & Ellesmere Railway, and, with the help of his long-standing friend and business partner Henry Robertson (1816-1888), the Liberal Member of Parliament for Shrewsbury, he formed a new company with the aim of completing a rail link from the Wrexham, Mold & Connah's Quay line at Wrexham to the Whitchurch, Ellesmere & Oswestry route at Ellesmere, the necessary Act of Parliament being obtained on 31st July, 1885.

The new scheme was very similar to the earlier proposals for a line from Wrexham to Bettisfield, although the junction with the Cambrian Railways would now be formed about two miles further west in order to serve the important intermediate station at Ellesmere.

The Wrexham & Ellesmere Act provided consent for a line running northwards from Ellesmere, via Overton and Bangor-on-Dee, and thence north-westwards to Wrexham. Capital of £180,000 in £10 shares was authorised, and a period of five years was allowed for completion of the works. The number of Directors was fixed at seven, the minimum qualification for Board membership being 40 shares.

Unfortunately, the Wrexham & Ellesmere scheme was brought before the investing public during a serious trade depression, which resulted in reduced coal and mineral traffic on the parent Wrexham, Mold & Connah's Quay line. There was little incentive for the promoters to begin work on the Ellesmere route at a time when their original line was under financial pressure, and in these circumstances there was no attempt to implement the Wrexham & Ellesmere scheme.

In 1888 the project suffered a cruel double blow when the death of Henry Robertson, on 22nd February, was followed just two days later by the death of Benjamin Piercy. The Wrexham & Ellesmere scheme was, as a result, again deferred.

In the meantime, the shifting sands of railway politics ensured that external parties would eventually come to the rescue of the Wrexham & Ellesmere project. As mentioned earlier, the Manchester, Sheffield & Lincolnshire Railway was keen to expand its influence towards Wales and the Welsh borders, and these ambitions were brought a step nearer on 31st March, 1890, when the Wrexham, Mold & Connah's Quay Railway opened a 4½ mile extension from Buckley Junction to the banks of the River Dee at Shotton; here, the WM&CQ line made an end-on junction with a new Manchester, Sheffield & Lincolnshire branch, which had opened to public traffic on the same day. The new line crossed the Dee by means of the massive Hawarden swing bridge, and it provided a direct link between the Cheshire Lines system at Chester and the WM&CQ route to Wrexham.

There was now considerable interest in the concept of a trunk line between Merseyside and South Wales that would be entirely independent of the existing route via Crewe, Shrewsbury, Hereford and Newport. A 'Standing Committee of Welsh Railways' had been in existence for several years, and in 1889 the possibility of a Welsh Railways Union was brought a step nearer with the successful passage through Parliament of a Welsh Railways Through Traffic Act.

Events were now moving rapidly, and in addition to the opening of the northwards extension of the Wrexham, Mold & Connah's Quay Railway there were plans for a further extension from Hawarden Bridge to Bidston, in the Wirral Peninsula.

The Wrexham, Mold & Connah's Quay Railway had earlier joined forces with the Wirral Railway to obtain an Act for such a line. But as neither of these companies had sufficient resources to build the Bidston extension, the Wirral Railway transferred its interests in the scheme to the Manchester, Sheffield & Lincolnshire company under the terms of the Wirral Railway Transfer Act of 12th August, 1889.

These events in the Deeside and Merseyside areas impinged directly on the still unrealised Wrexham & Ellesmere scheme. With Manchester, Sheffield &

Lincolnshire support, the Wrexham, Mold & Connah's Quay Railway had secured its northern links towards Birkenhead, Liverpool, Chester and Manchester, but, without the southern extension to Ellesmere, the ambitious Welsh Union route would simply peter out at Wrexham. For this reason, it remained of vital importance that the Wrexham & Ellesmere line should be built as the final link in a chain of connecting railways between South Wales and the populous industrial cities of north-western England.

An Agreement with the Great Western?

Perhaps surprisingly, the rival Great Western Railway also became involved in the Wrexham & Ellesmere scheme, its interest being prompted mainly by a desire to thwart London & North Western ambitions in the Welsh border area. At the same time, by apparently siding with the Manchester, Sheffield & Lincolnshire Railway, the Great Western may have hoped to be able to exert influence on the latter company - and thereby limit damage to its own legitimate interests in the Welsh borders.

Having obtained the necessary Act, the supporters of the scheme seemed in no hurry to begin construction, one difficulty being the inability of the three companies involved to reach full agreement on the next course of action. While it was generally agreed that the Wrexham & Ellesmere line would be worked by the Cambrian Railways, there was considerable indecision regarding the future ownership and status of the Wrexham, Mold & Connah's Quay line. At one time it was suggested that the latter route could be leased jointly by the Great Western and Manchester, Sheffield & Lincolnshire railways, while the MS&L company would be given running powers to Oswestry.

As a corollary of this scheme it was hoped that the Wrexham & Ellesmere line would itself be constructed jointly by the GWR, Manchester, Sheffield & Lincolnshire & Cambrian railways. In the event, full agreement could not be reached, and the Great Western eventually lost interest in the proposed new line. At the same time, there were problems concerning land acquisition, and this caused further delays to the Wrexham & Ellesmere project.

In retrospect, there must be at least a suspicion that the Great Western did not want the Wrexham and Ellesmere line to be built at all - it was, after all, a competing route that was expected to take local traffic from the Shrewsbury & Chester main line. Furthermore, it is inconceivable that the GWR would have let the Manchester, Sheffield & Lincolnshire Railway reach South Wales, and on reflection, it is hardly surprising that the three railway companies involved in the Ellesmere scheme should have failed to reach an amicable agreement.

Directors & Promoters: A Further Note

Henry Robertson, who, with Benjamin Piercy, appears to have been an important supporter of the proposed Wrexham to Ellesmere line, had started his career as an engineer, and by the 1850s he was acting in this capacity for the Shrewsbury & Chester, Shrewsbury & Birmingham and Shrewsbury & Hereford railways. Having prospered greatly during the railway boom of the 1840s he later branched out into mining and engineering, and soon acquired important interests in the Brymbo and Westminster collieries and the Ruabon Coal Company. It is of interest to note that this Scottish-born engineer was (with Frederick Peacock and Charles Beyer) a founder of Beyer, Peacock & Company, the locomotive builders of Gorton, Manchester.

Although initially well-disposed towards the GWR, Robertson later became an opponent of the Great Western monopoly position in the Welsh border industrial areas, and he supported several rival schemes.

Henry Robertson was undoubtedly one of the chief backers of the Wrexham, Mold & Connah's Quay Railway and the Wrexham & Ellesmere project, both of these lines being seen as transport outlets for the many collieries around Wrexham in which he was interested. He maintained his interests in Beyer, Peacock & Company for many years, and was also involved with the famous Brymbo Ironworks.

The career of Benjamin Piercy parallels that of Henry Robertson - both men being engineers who also saw the financial implications of railway-building and (one must suppose) share speculation. Benjamin Piercy started his career as an employee of Henry Robertson, and in later years he constructed railways in Italy and India. In an international context, Piercy's work in Italy was probably his greatest achievement in that the 300 or so miles of line constructed in that country helped to weld the disparate Italian states together into a unified nation.

William Davies, who had been involved in the early surveys for a line, from Wrexham to Bettisfield, was Benjamin Piercy's brother-in-law. He was clearly very close to Piercy, and had carried out work on several of Piercy's lines (including some of the Italian contracts). The employment of friends and relatives such as William Davies seems to have been a characteristic feature of Piercy's business activities, although, in a relatively small, closely-knit community such as Wrexham it would be unfair to see anything unduly sinister in any of this.

There were obvious suggestions that Benjamin Piercy would have welcomed a title to add further to his new-found status. One of Piercy's daughters actually married an Italian prince, and he was a personal friend of Guissepe Garibaldi - the hero of the Italian revolution. Cynics argued that no ordinary investor ever made a penny out of Benjamin Piercy's railway schemes, but there can be little doubt that the man himself was one of the most colourful railway promoters of his day!

George Owen, The Engineer

A.H. Aslett, Resident Engineer

Llewelyn Davies, Contractor

Howel Davies, Contractor

Portraits of key personalities involved in the construction of the Wrexham & Ellesmere Railway.
Wrexham Advertiser

Chapter Two

Construction and Opening of the Wrexham & Ellesmere Railway

With no real progress having been made following the deaths of Henry Robertson and Benjamin Piercy, the promoters of the Wrexham & Ellesmere Railway were obliged to seek powers for an extension of time for completion of the works, and by an Act of 10th August, 1888 the period for completion was extended to 31st July, 1893.

In the event, even this new deadline for completion proved insufficient, and on 22nd May, 1890, a further Act of Parliament provided an extra two years for completion until 31st July, 1895. On 14th May, 1895, the Wrexham & Ellesmere company obtained additional powers for the construction of a 31 chain north-to-west loop line at the Ellesmere end of the authorised route.

Boardroom Changes

The Wrexham & Ellesmere Railway Company retained its nominal independence, with its own Chairman, Board of Directors and officers. Most of these gentlemen were, nonetheless, acting for other interests, and a brief examination of their backgrounds serves only to underline the extent to which the Wrexham & Ellesmere scheme was a product of Manchester, Sheffield & Lincolnshire ambitions.

In the closing years of the 19th century the Wrexham & Ellesmere's Board of Directors included William Pollitt, James William Maclure, James Frederick Buckley and George Thomas Kenyon - the latter being the company's Chairman and the local Member of Parliament.

William Pollitt was General Manager of the Manchester, Sheffield & Lincolnshire Railway (which was officially re-named the Great Central Railway on 1st August, 1897) and Chairman of the Wrexham, Mold & Connah's Quay Railway. Similarly, his colleague James W. Maclure was a Director of both the MS&L, and Wrexham, Mold & Connah's Quay companies, and he had also secured a place on the Cambrian Railways Board; perhaps of equal significance he was a close friend of Sir Edward Watkin, the former MS&L Chairman.

James F. Buckley was, at that time, the Chairman of the Cambrian Railways, though it is interesting to note that his home was in Oldham (i.e. deep in Manchester, Sheffield & Lincolnshire territory).

Finally, George T. Kenyon, the Wrexham & Ellesmere Chairman, was a prominent local landowner with interests in various brickworks and other undertakings in the Wrexham area, including the Knowl Lane Brickworks, which was served by a branch of the Buckley Railway (later part of the Wrexham, Mold & Connah's Quay system).

Construction Begins

Eventually, after many delays, a contract for the construction of the Wrexham & Ellesmere Railway was belatedly let, the contractors being Messrs Howel & Llewelyn Davies Brothers of Wrexham. Davies Brothers offices were at 3-5 Hill Street, within yards of the proposed railway.

George Owen, the Cambrian Railways Engineer, was appointed Engineer-in-Chief for the new line, while plans and sections were prepared by J.F. Thomas of Wrexham; David Charles Jones was appointed Resident Engineer with day-to-day responsibility for the progress of the works.

When completed, the Wrexham & Ellesmere line would be worked as an integral part of the Cambrian Railways system, and in anticipation of the opening of the line the Cambrian ordered three 0-4-4 bogie tank locomotives for service on the new branch (*see Chapter Three*).

As a first step towards the construction of the long-hoped-for line to the south, the Wrexham, Mold & Connah's Quay Railway decided to build a brand new station at Wrexham, which would be on a site to the east of the original WM&CQ station and linked to it by a 70 chain connecting line. Parliamentary consent was obtained for this new project by an Act of 18th August, 1882. The new station, which would in future be known as Wrexham Central to distinguish it from the other WM&CQ station at Wrexham Exchange, was approached by an underline bridge beneath the GWR main line, and many old buildings had to be cleared before construction could begin.

The new connection in Wrexham was opened on 1st November, 1887, on which day Wrexham Central station was also brought into use. The line was originally single track, though its bridges were wide enough to accommodate a double line of rails; the ruling gradient was 1 in 100. A second line of rails between Wrexham Exchange and Wrexham Central was brought into use on 1st September, 1888, though the original wood and corrugated iron station buildings at Wrexham Central, which were supposed to be only temporary, were not replaced.

In physical terms the construction of the Wrexham and Ellesmere line presented few problems. The branch ran through gently rolling agricultural countryside with a maximum elevation of a little over 300 ft at the Ellesmere end, falling steadily to around 100 ft above mean sea level around Bangor-on-Dee; there were no major obstacles *en route* apart from the River Dee crossing at Bangor. At its northern end the new line would make use of the newly-opened Wrexham Central station, with cross-platform interchange facilities between the Cambrian and Wrexham, Mold & Connah's Quay lines.

The first sod of the Wrexham & Ellesmere Railway was ceremonially cut at Wrexham on 11th July, 1892, and the townsfolk turned out in large numbers to witness these historic proceedings. It was agreed that the ceremony would be performed by Mrs Kenyon, the wife of George Kenyon MP of Penley - the Wrexham & Ellesmere Chairman. The town was decorated with flags and bunting to mark the great occasion, and church bells were rung at intervals throughout the day.

CONSTRUCTION AND OPENING

At around noon, a special train arrived in the platforms at Central station, and a procession then formed up behind the town band. Richard William Evans, the Mayor of Wrexham, rode in a carriage with Mr and Mrs Kenyon, and the procession included 15 teams of horses pulling wagons piled high with rails and constructional materials.

Having reached the construction site near the present Caia Road, the procession halted while Mrs Kenyon dexterously made the first incisions in the ground, and placed the first sod in a highly-decorated ornamental wheelbarrow that had been specially made for the ceremony. The first sods being turned, the official party adjourned to the Wynnstay Hotel, where Mrs Kenyon was presented with a miniature silver wheelbarrow in recognition of her part in the ceremony.

Over 600 men were soon hard at work on the railway. Construction depots were established at Caia Road and Abenbury - the latter site being used for quarrying and brick making by Messrs Davies Brothers.

The new railway wrought great changes in Wrexham, where huge swathes of existing property were swept away to make room for the Wrexham & Ellesmere line. Much of this property was in poor condition, the area involved being a somewhat deprived working class district with many slum houses. This may, at least in part, have been a result of what today might be called 'planning blight' - the railway had of course been under serious consideration for no less than 20 years!

Interestingly, Benjamin Piercy had been assiduously buying up property along the proposed route of the line for several years, and this land had passed into the control of his Trustees after his death in 1888. It remains a matter of conjecture why Mr Piercy should have followed this course of action. On one level, he may have been simply investing in a speculative (but ultimately profitable) venture, but it is conceivable that he was also hoping to expedite the building of his railway - self interest therefore coalesced with the public good in a way that made everybody happy. Whatever the original motive, the fact remained that Benjamin Piercy's earlier actions enabled the Wrexham & Ellesmere Railway to purchase much of the necessary land from the Trustees of the Piercy Estate, and this undoubtedly helped to bring the scheme to a successful conclusion.

Some parcels of land in the Wrexham area were not in the hands of the Piercy Trustees, and in such cases the railway builders faced potential problems. One land owner - Mr F.W. Soames, proprietor of the brewery in Mount Street - was reluctant to sell; he suggested that, rather than relinquish just part of the site, he would prefer to sell the entire brewery. Later, however, he relented, and the railway company was able to obtain the narrow strip of land that would be needed along the southern edge of the premises.

Considerable demolition was necessary in the Brook Street area between Vicarage Hill and Town Hill, while a complex of 18th century houses in Yorkshire Square (off Tuttle Street) were obliterated. The cottages in question were among the most noisome slums in Wrexham, and their removal was perhaps no real loss. Elsewhere, further houses were demolished in the Mount Street and Mount Pleasant districts.

The contractors' locomotive *Dorothy*, built by Manning, Wardle in 1886, was used during the construction of the Wrexham & Ellesmere Railway.
Denbighshire Record Office

CONSTRUCTION AND OPENING

The 0-4-0ST *Cymro*, another of the contractors' fleet of locomotives used during construction of the railway.

Contractors' Locomotives used by Davies Brothers during construction of the Wrexham & Ellesmere Railway

Engine	Notes
Bantam	Four-wheeled coupled tank, no other details. Later used at Abenbury brickworks.
Cymro	0-4-0ST, outside cylinders 10 in. x 14 in., unknown builder, obtained from Cudsworth & Johnson, machinery dealers, Wrexham.
Dorothy	0-4-0ST, outside cylinders 8 in. x 14 in., built by Manning, Wardle & Co. Works No. 977 in 1886, previously owned by Naylor Bros, contractors.
Penwylly	0-6-0ST, outside cylinders 13½ in., believed built by Fox, Walker & Co., previously owned by the contractor John Dickson.
Weedon	0-6-0ST, inside cylinders 12 in. x 17 in., built by Manning, Wardle & Co. No. 976 in 1886, previously owned by Naylor Bros, contractors.

All except *Dorothy* were offered for sale at an auction held in the yard adjoining Davies Bros' Abenbury brickworks on 1st June, 1897, on the completion of the contract. The auctioneer was G.N. Dixon.

Source Industrial Locomotive Society

A contractors' locomotive at work, possibly at Cooke's Weir *circa* 1892. The lcomomotive appears to be *Dorothy*. Cooke's Weir, to the south of Wrexham near Hightown Halt, was sometimes known as 'Cooper's Bridge'; here, the railway was carried across the River Gwenfro.
Denbighshire Record Office

The line under construction at Kings Mill. *Denbighshire Record Office*

A temporary timber trestle viaduct was built over the Clywedog at Abenbury during the construction of the W&E line. Note the derelict Abenbury forge, visible to the left of the picture.
Denbighshire Record Office

Kings Mill viaduct shortly after completion.
Denbighshire Record Office

A contractors' crane is hauled by the steam road locomotive *Demon* during construction of the Wrexham & Ellesmere Railway. It is believed that this photograph was taken *circa* 1893/4 at the junction of the Derby and Hightown roads.
Denbighshire Record Office

A steam navvy is captured in this view taken near Bangor-on-Dee. *Flintshire Record Office*

Two views of demolition of houses in the Mount Street area of Wrexham during construction of the railway. Mount House is seen in the view above. *(Both) Denbighshire Record Office*

This view shows the Old Vicarage shortly before its demolition. Although sold in 1880, the building remained in derelict condition for several years.
Denbighshire Record Office

Another casualty in the name of late 19th century progress was the Old Vicarage at the top of what is now Vicarage Hill. This two-and-a-half storey brick house had ceased to be used as a vicarage in the 1820s, but it was of architectural interest and should perhaps have been preserved. On a footnote, it is worth mentioning that the hymn *From Greenland's Icy Mountains* was written in the Old Vicarage by Bishop R. Heber (1783-1826) while on a visit to his father-in-law, Dean Shipley.

Construction proceeded satisfactorily during 1893 and 1894, though there were at one time problems with the supply of girders for the Dee viaduct at Bangor. George Owen, the line's Engineer, decided that the river would be crossed by a 195 ft span, and the Pearson & Knowles Coal & Iron Company of Warrington was engaged to make the necessary girders; this river bridge would have one of the longest single spans in the country at that time. In addition to the bridge itself, the railway builders were also faced with the construction of a ¾ mile embankment on the north bank of the Dee, which would be pierced by three underline bridges to allow the release of flood water during the winter months .

The earthworks were well-advanced by the early months of 1895, and in February 1895 the *Wrexham Argus* was able to report that the works on the Wrexham & Ellesmere Railway (W&E) were 'progressing' despite the 'changeable state of the weather'; the paper added, however, that the railway would not be ready in time to carry passengers 'in connection with the Wynnstay Hunt Steeplechase Meeting', which would be held on 19th April.

A few weeks later, in March 1895, the same journal was able to print the following brief progress report:

> At the recent meeting of the Wrexham & Ellesmere Railway Company, it was stated that Mr William Pollitt and other Directors had gone over the line, that the work of the contractors had been well done so far as it went, and that if due energy was shown the line ought to be opened for goods traffic in a couple months.

On a sad note, the construction of the line had been marred, to some extent, by the death of the original Resident Engineer, Mr D.C. Jones, who the *Border Counties Advertizer* had described as 'a young man of great ability'. Mr Jones was replaced by James Wilkinson of Oswestry, who held the appointment on a temporary basis until he was himself replaced by A.H. Aslett, the nephew of the Cambrian Railways General Manager.

The First Passenger-Carrying Train

The railway was more or less complete by the summer of 1895, its earthworks and permanent way being in place throughout the 12½ mile route from Wrexham to Ellesmere. Indeed, the works were so advanced that it was possible for the conveyance of passengers to take place when a special excursion train was run from Wrexham to Ellesmere on 2nd July, 1895.

The excursion was an Anglican Church outing, and over 90 passengers took advantage of this unique opportunity to travel over the as yet un-opened line to

Ellesmere. The train comprised four Wrexham, Mold & Connah's Quay short-wheelbase passenger vehicles and a locomotive supplied by the contractors. The trip was arranged as a collaborative effort between the Vicar of Wrexham and the line's contractors - Howel Davies and his brother Llewelyn.

Something of the flavour of the occasion is captured by the following extract from the August 1895 edition of the *Wrexham Argus*:

> At the invitation of the Vicar, churchwardens, and sidesmen of Wrexham, the members of the Parish Church choir and bellringers, together with a number of friends, visited Ellesmere on the 2nd ultimo, by the new railway. By the kindness of the contractors, Messrs Howel and Llewelyn Davies, a party numbering about ninety left the Central Station shortly after two o'clock, in a train of four coaches, with guard complete, furnished by the Wrexham, Mold & Connah's Quay Railway Company and drawn by one of the contractors' engines.
>
> This was the first passenger train to make the journey over the new railway, and visitors were much pleased with the views of the country which were opened to them.
>
> At Ellesmere, a service was held in the Oteley Chapel, conducted by the Reverend Canon Fletcher and the Reverend Clement Thompson. Mr Pullein, organist of Wrexham Parish Church, presided at the organ. After service, the Wrexham ringers rang a quarter peal of Grandsire Triples, and the rest of the visitors entertained themselves as best they could, for the weather was not favourable . . . subsequently, an excellent tea was provided by Mr and Mrs Knight, at the Bridgewater Hotel, when Canon Fletcher presided.
>
> After tea, the Chairman proposed votes of thanks to Mr Howel Davies, who had so kindly brought them down, to the Vicar of Ellesmere for the use of the church, organ, and the bells; to the Mayor and Mayoress of Wrexham for their presence, to Mr William Overton for his attendance, and the Alderman and Mrs R.W. Evans for their many kindnesses.

Several further speeches were then made, one of the speakers being the Mayor of Wrexham, who referred enthusiastically to his journey over the new railway:

> The Mayor (Mr Charles Murlees) responded to the vote of thanks on behalf of the Mayoress and himself. He had had a new experience, in having come to Ellesmere by train, and so astonished were some of his Ellesmere friends to learn that he had come by train, that some of them had gone to the station to see the carriages!

The contractors, in responding to the Mayor's speech, alluded to the pleasure that the trip had given them; Howel Davies hoped that the homeward journey to Wrexham would 'be performed as safely as the outward one had been', and he then referred to the importance of the Wrexham & Ellesmere line, which would form 'an important link in a great Welsh railway development'.

The speeches having at last ended, the company dispersed, the Wrexham party making their way to the station. The northwards journey was rapidly accomplished, and such was the novelty of the occasion that numerous groups of interested spectators had gathered at various bridges and other points to watch the inaugural special. The event had, by that time, developed into a sort of semi-official Opening Day, and the *Wrexham Argus*, report noted that many of the lineside crowds 'cheered the unusual spectacle very heartily'.

Completion and Opening of the Wrexham & Ellesmere Railway

The trip to Ellesmere was clearly a great publicity coup for the new railway, but the route could not be properly opened for public traffic until it had passed its compulsory Board of Trade inspection. This matter was in hand by the summer, and after an exchange of correspondence between the railway company and the Board of Trade it was arranged for the government inspection to take place on 24th September, 1895, the Inspecting Officer being Lieutenant-Colonel H.A. Yorke of the Royal Engineers.

The Board of Trade inspection took place, as planned, on 24th September, 1895. The BoT Inspector was, in general, well-satisfied with the strength and stability of the new works - the Dee bridge, in particular, being specifically praised as a 'very fine work' of civil engineering. Elsewhere, Colonel Yorke pointed out that a pedestrian footbridge was required at the junction station at Ellesmere.

The inspection did not pass entirely without problems because the signal box at Wrexham Central station had burned down immediately before Colonel Yorke's visit. Nevertheless, the Wrexham & Ellesmere route was now ready for public traffic, the first day of operation being scheduled for Saturday 2nd November, 1895.

Meanwhile, the passage of the Board of Trade inspection train had itself attracted a measure of local interest, and in October the *Wrexham Argus* published the following short report:

> OUR LOCAL RAILWAYS - Lieutenant-Colonel Yorke, Board of Trade Inspector, passed over the line from Ellesmere to Wrexham on the 24th ult., tried all the bridges and viaducts and passed them and the line as being very satisfactory.
>
> With Lieutenant-Colonel Yorke were Mr Aslett, General Manager of the Cambrian Railways; Mr George Owen, CE; Mr A.H. Aslett; Mr Dutton, signal contractor of Worcester; Mr Saunders, telegraph and telephone contractor, Cardiff; and Mr Howel Davies (Messrs Davies Brothers), permanent way contractors.
>
> On the following day he made an inspection of the Central Station, but owing to the destruction of the main signal box by fire a few days before, he was unable to complete his inspection. It is expected that the box will have been re-constructed in about a fortnight, when the line will be ready for opening.

Having passed its Board of Trade inspection, the railway was opened on 2nd November. No official celebrations were planned, perhaps because the recent special excursion to Ellesmere had already enabled the Mayor of Wrexham and other local dignitaries to travel over the new line. On the other hand, the fact that Opening Day would be a Saturday ensured that large numbers of ordinary people who would otherwise have been at work were able to ride over the branch on its official first day of operation.

As might be expected, the local press turned out in force to record the day's events, the Opening Day being well-covered by the *Wrexham Argus*, the *Border Counties Advertizer*, and the *Wrexham Advertiser* - the latter paper even produced a special illustrated supplement in celebration of the event.

The day's activities commenced at the northern end of the line, where A.H. Aslett, the Resident Engineer, prepared to board the first scheduled up service

An early view of Cambrian Railways 0-4-4T No. 3 and its train at Wrexham Central.
Revd Alan Cliff

The same locomotive is seen in a staged photograph at the newly-completed Marchwiel station.
R.W. Miller Collection

CONSTRUCTION AND OPENING

from Wrexham Central to Ellesmere in company with a small group of first-day travellers. The train itself consisted of five green and white Cambrian Railways coaches and one of the new 'No. 3' class 0-4-4Ts that had recently been built by Nasmyth, Wilson & Company for service over the Wrexham & Ellesmere Railway.

The first southbound working was described as follows by the *Border Counties Advertizer*:

> The first train left Wrexham at 8.10 am. It consisted of an engine, five coaches and guard's van. Mr A.H. Aslett, the Resident Engineer, was on the engine, and Inspectors Edwards (Cambrian Railways) and Powell (Wrexham, Mold & Connah's Quay Railway) were also on the train.
>
> Twenty eight passengers went from Wrexham by the train. A large number of fog signals were laid upon the rails near the Central Station, and a number of rockets were also discharged. Great interest was shown in the event, large crowds of people having congregated along the line.
>
> At Ellesmere a large number of people had assembled on the platforms and on the railway bridge to watch the arrival and departure of the first trains.
>
> After the 8.53 am from Oswestry had cleared the station the 'new train' ran from its sidings alongside the down platform, and very soon nearly forty passengers had taken their seats for their first trip along the new line.

Having run-round its train, the 0-4-4T (presumably the same engine that had brought the up working into Ellesmere) left with the 9.05 am down service, and reached Overton-on-Dee in eight minutes. Here, a number of extra passengers joined the train, and on arrival in Wrexham large crowds greeted this first down working.

Although no formal ceremonies had been specifically arranged, the first day developed a momentum of its own as more and more people turned up at the stations to ride on the first trains. Wrexham Central, Ellesmere and the intermediate stations were crowded with sightseers, while over 400 people booked tickets from Wrexham. The following statistics were provided by the *Wrexham Advertiser* in its Wednesday 9th November edition:

> 410 passengers were booked from Wrexham. They left for the following places: - Ninety-six for Marchwiel, ninety-seven for Bangor-on-Dee, sixty-six for Overton-on-Dee, one hundred and fifty-one for Ellesmere and twenty-four places beyond Ellesmere, including Oswestry.
>
> The best trains were the 1.35 pm, 3.45 pm and 8.30 pm, the former carrying 142 passengers, and the others 109 and 111 respectively. The number of passengers booked from Oswestry was 128, and from Ellesmere fifty-two, and with those from intermediate stations the total number of passengers exceeded 200.

One of the highlights of the day was the passage of a Manchester, Sheffield & Lincolnshire special which, according to the *Border Counties Advertizer*, was 'drawn by their latest engine, one weighing over eighty-eight tons'; this special service carried a large number of specially-invited dignitaries from the Manchester, Sheffield & Lincolnshire Railway and its subsidiaries - a full guest list being furnished by the *Wrexham Advertiser*:

These drawings were published in the *Wrexham Advertiser* on the opening of the railway. Above we see Bangor-on-Dee station showing its wooden construction, and below the Dee bridge near Bangor.

Wrexham Advertiser

CONSTRUCTION AND OPENING

The party included Mr William Pollitt, General Manager of the Manchester, Sheffield & Lincolnshire Railway Company, a Director of the Wrexham & Ellesmere, and Chairman of the Wrexham, Mold & Connah's Quay Railway companies; Mr Meldrum, General Manager of the Cheshire Lines; Mr Thomas Cartwright, General Manager of the Wrexham, Mold & Connah's Quay Railway; Mr George Owen, Engineer of the Cambrian and Wrexham & Ellesmere railways; Messrs Llewelyn and Howel Davies, the contractors of the new line; Mr A.H. Aslett, Mr W.W. Strover, and Mr Pollitt Junior.

At Ellesmere, the official party was further augmented when George Kenyon the Wrexham & Ellesmere Chairman, James Buckley the Cambrian Railways Chairman, and a number of other friends, relatives and officials joined the MS&L train. The entire party then travelled back to Wrexham, where lunch was served aboard the train as it stood in the Central station.

The sight of this gleaming main line train, thronged with almost the entire upper management of five railway companies, would probably have been the main event of the day for late-Victorian railway enthusiasts, though further excitement was provided later in the afternoon when a heavy excursion set out from Oswestry for Wrexham. The latter service was ostensibly provided in connection with a football match, but on ascending the rising gradients between Bangor-on-Dee and Wrexham the locomotive failed, and long delays ensued until a relief engine could be found. At length, an elderly Wrexham, Mold & Connah's Quay tank locomotive was sent out to collect the stranded excursion - which eventually reached Wrexham behind this unexpected motive power (albeit too late for the football match!).

Some Details of the Line

The new line was single track throughout between Wrexham Central and Ellesmere, with crossing loops at the intermediate stations. At Ellesmere, the branch joined the Oswestry, Ellesmere & Whitchurch route by means of a triangular junction, which would allow direct running between Wrexham and Ellesmere for local trains, and between Wrexham and Oswestry for through workings from the North of England to the Cambrian main line. The original stations between Ellesmere and Wrexham were at Overton-on-Dee, Bangor-on-Dee and Marchwiel.

The new railway was built as cheaply as possible, its stations being little more than large wooden shacks, while the timber goods sheds were of particularly flimsy construction. The track layouts at the intermediate stations were, nevertheless, laid out on a generous scale, with lengthy crossing loops that were clearly designed in anticipation of an extensive traffic in coal and minerals between the industrial areas of Northern England and the Welsh coal fields.

The principal engineering works included the 66 yard Dee viaduct and its associated approach works, the Willow Road and Town Hill viaducts at Wrexham which had a combined length of over 130 yards, and the Kings Mill viaduct between Marchwiel and Wrexham, which had a length of 84 yards.

Elsewhere, there were a number of smaller under or overbridges, together with various cuttings and embankments along the route of the 12½ mile line.

The ordinary overbridges, were mainly of brick or stone construction, and built to accommodate a second line of rails in case future traffic needs should ever justify the doubling of all or part of the route.

The route dropped from Wrexham towards the Dee viaduct, the gradients on this northern section being from 1 in 65 to 1 in 304, with quite long stretches of 1 in 301 and 1 in 86. Thereafter, the line climbed out of the Dee Valley at 1 in 84/85 and 1 in 101 before dropping towards Ellesmere at 1 in 1,277.

The line was worked as an integral part of the Cambrian Railways, all necessary locomotives, staff, rolling stock, tickets, and other items and equipment being provided by the Cambrian company under the terms of an operating agreement dated 22nd September, 1891 whereby the latter company secured 55 per cent of the gross receipts.

In physical terms, the Wrexham & Ellesmere line transformed a considerable part of Wrexham. As we have seen, the railway cut through an area of run-down working class housing, and quite apart from the demolition of property the line also brought in its wake various new road schemes; Vicarage Hill, for example, was turned into a link road between Priory Street and Brook Street, while Caia Road - which had hitherto been little more than a rough track to Caia Farm - was transformed into a residential street flanking the new Wrexham & Ellesmere Railway's goods yard.

For much of its length through the built-up areas of Wrexham the railway ran on continuous viaducts or embankments, while the Caia Road goods yard was constructed on raised and levelled ground. Nearby, the course of the River Gwenfro was artificially straightened or culverted in connection with the new line.

Moving eastwards, Messrs Davies brothers seem to have retained their depot and brick works at Abenbury, together with a private siding connection from the Wrexham & Ellesmere main line. The contractors had employed their own locomotives, rolling stock and steam cranes during the construction of the railway, and much of this equipment was moved to the Abenbury site after the completion of the works.

Most of the equipment and rolling stock was auctioned at Abenbury in June 1897, though it is believed that one of the contractors' locomotives was kept at the brick works for use as a private shunter; the engine in question was a typical late Victorian contractors' 0-4-0 tank known as *Bantam*.

Further details of Abenbury siding and brick works will be given in *Chapter Five*, but it may be worth mentioning here that the 1898 edition of the 25 inch Ordnance Survey map shows the layout of Messrs Davies Brothers' former construction depot in detail; three dead-end sidings are shown, one of which may have served an engine shed. There is an 'Old Quarry' that must have been used during the construction of the line, together with several buildings and at least nine brick kilns and a clay pit.

The facilities at Abenbury were subsequently modified for use as a stone yard and brick works, but one of the sidings was retained for brick traffic, and this became the first private siding on the Wrexham & Ellesmere line. Davies Brothers continued to manufacture bricks in the Abenbury works after the cessation of the railway contract, and bricks bearing the inscription 'Abenbury Brick Works - Davies Brothers' can still be found in the Wrexham area.

Chapter Three

Developments during the Cambrian and Great Western Periods

The newly-opened railway formed part of a comprehensive transport system which, by the 1890s, reached into almost every corner of the land. The railways were at the very peak of their power, and at a time when great companies such as the Midland and London & North Western railways held an undisputed monopoly of land transport, they seemed to be the ultimate symbol of Britain's world-beating industrial technology. At a time when local communities such as Marchwiel and Overton-on-Dee still moved at the speed of a horse, the familiar steam railways were the fastest, safest and most efficient means of transport on earth.

The various railway companies expressed their individuality in a number of different ways - the most obvious of which, to the travelling public, being the liveries of locomotives and rolling stock. The Cambrian Railways engines seen on the Wrexham & Ellesmere line sported a lined black livery, with linear decoration in grey and red, while passenger rolling stock was green below waist level and white above (later changed to all-over green); freight vehicles were painted dark grey with the company's name displayed in white letters.

On arrival at Wrexham Central, these distinctive trains terminated alongside the Wrexham, Mold & Connah's Quay platforms, and late-Victorian travellers would then have noticed that the WM&CQ engines were entirely different - being, for the most part, saddle tanks painted in lined 'Indian red' livery; the WM&CQ coaches were purple-brown with white upper panels until about 1900, after which they became dark brown all over.

Although, as far as ordinary travellers were concerned the Wrexham & Ellesmere line appeared to be an integral part of the Cambrian Railways system, the W&E company was, in reality, dominated by the Great Central Railway (GCR). By the turn of the the last century, most Wrexham & Ellesmere Directors were Great Central nominees, and the company's registered headquarters was in Marylebone station. The GCR company treated the Wrexham & Ellesmere line as an extension of the Wrexham, Mold & Connah's Quay line - the latter having passed into full Great Central control on 1st January, 1905.

On the other hand, there was no attempt to operate the WM&CQ and W&E sections as one continuous line, and through passengers could not avoid the change of trains at Wrexham Central. It is conceivable that the Great Central would have considered outright purchase of the W&E, but the Cambrian was never likely to relinquish its own legitimate interests in this Welsh border line.

Locomotives & Train Services in the Early Twentieth Century

As we have seen, the Cambrian company ordered three four-coupled tank locomotives for work on the Wrexham & Ellesmere line in the 1890s. These engines were built by Nasmyth, Wilson & Company, the initial order for three

Cambrian Railways 'No. 3' class 0-4-4T No. 5 in original 1895 condition.

R.W. Miller Collection

In this view Cambrian Railways 'No. 3' class 0-4-4T No. 7 has had an extension fitted to its bunker to increase the coal capacity. The vehicle to the left appears to be a GWR auto-trailer (or steam railmotor).

locomotives being completed in 1895. As originally planned, the new engines would have been 4-4-0Ts but, at an early stage, the plans were modified to the 0-4-4T configuration.

Three more engines were added to the class in 1899, and the six 0-4-4Ts (known as the 'No. 3' class) worked mainly on the Wrexham & Ellesmere and Dolgelley lines. These bogie tank locomotives carried the numbers 3, 5 and 7 (Works Nos. 460, 461 and 462 respectively) and 8, 9 and 21 (Works Nos. 558, 559 and 560).

The 'No. 3' class 0-4-4Ts were of conventional appearance, being generally similar to other 0-4-4Ts designed for passenger service on various lines at that time. They had 17 in. x 24 in. inside cylinders and 5 ft 3 in. coupled wheels; their only unusual feature were their cabside windows, which were of the circular 'port hole' type. Some further details are given below:

Trailing wheels	3 ft 1½ in.
Weight	45 tons 9 cwt
Water capacity	1,200 gallons
Combined wheelbase	5 ft 3 in. + 7 ft 3½ in. + 7 ft 5 in.
Boiler Pressure	160 lb. per square inch
Total heating surface	920.1 square feet

The 'No. 3' class engines were taken over by the Great Western in 1922, but four were immediately withdrawn, leaving only Nos. 3 and 8 in service. Carrying the GWR numbers 10 and 19 respectively, they survived until 1932 - their final duties being on the Cambrian coast line, rather than the Wrexham & Ellesmere branch for which they had originally been built.

Other locomotives used on the Wrexham & Ellesmere line in pre-Grouping days included Cambrian Sharp, Stewart 2-4-0s and 0-6-0 goods engines, 50 ft turntables being available at Ellesmere and Wrexham Central to obviate tender-first operation when tender engines were used on the line.

Representing an older generation of Cambrian Railways motive power, Sharp, Stewart 2-4-0 No. 56 (ex-*Whittington*), dating from 1865, was used on the Wrexham & Ellesmere line in 1911; by that time, the engine had been rebuilt as a side tank for use on local passenger services.

Freight services were worked by the well known Cambrian Sharp, Stewart 'Queen' class, and other 0-6-0s. The Cambrian had 23 'Sharpies', several of which had been acquired from the Oswestry & Newtown Railway or other constituent companies, they had 16 in. x 24 in. cylinders and 4 ft 6 in. wheels. Like most Cambrian Railways locomotives, some of these goods engines had a long life, the last one in service being No. 9, which was withdrawn (as GWR No. 908) in 1947. In Cambrian days, all of these engines were painted black with yellow and red lining.

Although many of the Cambrian vehicles were six-wheelers, there were also a number of bogie coaches. Some of the trains seen on the Wrexham & Ellesmere line were through workings to or from the Great Central system, and photographic evidence shows that GCR coaches were sometimes attached to normal Cambrian services. Conversely, Cambrian vehicles worked through to Manchester or other destinations over the Cheshire Lines Committee system.

This 2-4-0 locomotive was built by Sharp, Stewart in 1865 as No. 56 and originally carried the name *Whittington*. This photograph was taken at Oswestry in 1891, the engine had been reboilered the previous year. It is conceivable that the engine may have worked on the W&E line in its original condition, although it did not become a regular branch engine until 1911.

R.W. Miller Collection

In 1907 No. 56 was converted to a 2-4-0 side tank for work on short stopping trains along the Cambrian Coast line from Penmaenpool. In 1911 it was transferred to the Wrexham & Ellesmere line to work motor-coach trains. The Cambrian's only motor coach is coupled to the engine.

R.W. Miller Collection

Cambrian Railways 0-6-0 No. 48, a Sharp, Stewart six-coupled tender engine dating from 1873, originally worked on the Mid-Wales Railway as MWR No. 9. The engine became GWR No. 908 and was withdrawn in 1938. In its last years the engine was based at Oswestry for local branch duties.
S.C. Jenkins/Lens of Sutton Collection

Cambrian Railways 0-6-0 No. 14, built by Sharp, Stewart in 1875 (Works No. 2511), became No. 898 after the Grouping. This locomotive was originally built for the Furness Railway, but it was never delivered, and was purchased instead by the Cambrian Railways in 1878.
S.C. Jenkins/Lens of Sutton Collection

Wrexham Central in 1904 looking towards Ellesmere. A Great Central Railway (ex-WM&CQ) train is on the left, while a three-coach Cambrian train is at the far end of the platform. St Giles' church looms prominently in the background. *R.W. Miller Collection*

'Seaham' class 2-4-0T No. 58 was built by Sharp, Stewart in 1866. The driving wheels were of 4 ft 6 in. diameter, and the leading radial wheels were 3 ft 0 in. The 'Seaham' class consisted of three engines and a number of modifications were made over the years. In 1910, sister engine No. 59 was used on the Wrexham & Ellesmere Railway. After absorption into the GWR the three engines were rebuilt at Swindon, Nos. 58 and 59 just survived into the Nationalised era. They were withdrawn in April 1948. No. 58 was known as *Gladys* until the early years of the 20th century.

Push-pull operation was employed on the Wrexham & Ellesmere branch from an early date, and in Cambrian days a bogie push-pull trailer was specially constructed from two old six-wheelers for service on the line; motive power was provided by one of the long-lived Cambrian 'Seaham' class 2-4-0Ts, which had been fitted-up with suitable push-pull control equipment.

The original train service provided around five to six trains in each direction between Wrexham and Ellesmere. In 1900, for example, there were five workings in each direction, with up services from Wrexham at 9.55 am, 1.35, 3.35, 7.15 and 9.15 pm and down workings from Ellesmere at 9.05 am, 12.05, 2.20, 3.55 and 5.55 pm. In the summer, the line carried through trains from Manchester to Chester to the Cambrian Coast resorts, one of which was the regular 11.18 am from Chester (Liverpool Road) to Aberystwyth, which ran non-stop between Wrexham Central and Oswestry, taking the west arm of the triangle at Ellesmere between Ellesmere North and West junctions.

At the end of the late Victorian period, this through working normally consisted of a 'first and third lavatory coach', which left Manchester Central at 10.09 am and travelled via Chester (Liverpool Road), Connah's Quay and Wrexham to Oswestry, where it was attached to the 12.20 pm Cambrian service from Whitchurch to Aberystwyth. In the opposite direction the return working left Aberystwyth at 12.05 pm, and was detached at Ellesmere; the through portion went forward to Wrexham as the 3.15 pm service to Wrexham, enabling through travellers to reach Manchester Central by 5.30 pm.

The Aberystwyth through trains originated on the Manchester, Sheffield & Lincolnshire (later Great Central) system, and, as such, they were perhaps the one tangible result of the MS&L company's earlier interest in the Wrexham & Ellesmere scheme. Additionally, some through goods traffic was carried over the Wrexham & Ellesmere line, and in this context it is interesting to note that the Cambrian Railways was granted through running powers for goods only over the Wrexham, Mold & Connah's Quay line as far as Brymbo South Junction.

In general, however, the Wrexham & Ellesmere line was never developed as part of a through route between England and Wales. The reasons for this were, quite simply, that the connecting lines on this through Great Central-Cambrian route were predominantly single track, and the companies involved were unwilling to expend vast sums in bringing them up to main line standards. Furthermore, the Great Western and LNWR companies could easily undercut the rival railways, and although their lines were in fact longer, the big companies retained their monopolies of traffic to and from South Wales.

There was, nevertheless, at least some attempt to encourage what today would be called 'leisure travel' between Wales and the populous cities of Liverpool and Manchester. On Fridays and Saturdays, for example, Great Central stations in the Manchester district issued 10- and 11-day excursion tickets to and from the Cambrian Railways system via Wrexham and Ellesmere. Similar ticketing arrangements were available from Great Central stations in the Humberside area, while half-day tickets were available on Mondays, Fridays and Saturdays from Merseyside to and from Wrexham and Ellesmere.

The Cambrian also did much to stimulate holiday and leisure travel and, for many years, first, second and third class tourist tickets were advertised from 'all

This postcard of Ellesmere station looking east towards Whitchurch was posted in 1913.

John Alsop Collection

DEVELOPMENTS DURING THE CAMBRIAN AND GWR PERIODS

Road competition: The Wrexham & District Electric Tramways (later the Wrexham & District Transport Co.) introduced local bus services in 1913, and a service was soon in operation between Wrexham and Overton using mainly Daimler vehicles (*see below*). The street tramway was abandoned in 1927, by which time the Wrexham to Overton service had been extended to Ellesmere in competition with the railway. These two views are reproduced from period postcards, the tram in the view above is seen in Brook Street. *S.C. Jenkins/Lens of Sutton Collection*

0-4-4T No. No. 5 waits to depart from Ellesmere with a Wrexham train c.1914. J.A. Peden

Ellesmere station, looking east towards Whitchurch in Cambrian days. Note the original tapered glass platform lamps, and the large number of milk churns. S.C. Jenkins Collection

the principal-stations in England' to destinations in North and Central Wales; these tickets were available for two calendar months via a variety of routes.

Although a small amount of extra traffic flowed over the Wrexham & Ellesmere route as a result of Cambrian and Great Central marketing initiatives, the W&E line remained a predominantly localised route. In this context it should be mentioned that Wrexham was, for many years, regarded as the commercial centre for a large area of North Wales and the inhabitants of small communities such as Bangor-on-Dee would obviously have used the railway for shopping trips and similar journeys. At the same time, the Wrexham & Ellesmere route served the needs of local industries such as Elson brickworks near Ellesmere, and the Wrexham Brick & Tile Company at Kings Mill - both of these firms being served directly by private siding connections.

World War I and the Grouping

Having failed to become part of a significant long distance through route for coal and holiday traffic, the Wrexham & Ellesmere line settled down to become a local branch line, serving the transport needs of local communities such as Marchwiel and Overton. In an attempt to stimulate further passenger traffic the Cambrian Railways (which continued to work the line although the Wrexham & Ellesmere company remained nominally independent) opened new halts at Sesswick, near Bangor-on-Dee, and at Trench, near Ellesmere, in October 1913 and December 1914 respectively.

The line became particularly busy during World War I, when large army camps were set up at various places served by the Cambrian Railways - notably at Park Hall, near Oswestry, at the western end of the Oswestry, Ellesmere & Whitchurch line. These establishments generated much extra passenger traffic over all parts of the largely single track Cambrian system, while at the same time the railway was struggling to move vast quantities of coal for industrial and naval use.

Much of this wartime coal traffic was sent northwards along the Mid-Wales line via Llanidloes, and thence through Oswestry to Ellesmere, Wrexham, Chester and the Cheshire Lines Committee, while in the reverse direction an endless procession of empty trains flowed southwards along the same single lines. These wartime coal trains were popularly known as 'Jellicoe Specials' after Admiral Sir John Jellicoe, the Commander-in-Chief of the Grand Fleet.

Ironically, the revolutionary 'Dreadnought' battleships of the Grand Fleet were powered by oil-fired steam turbines; similarly, the Navy's latest cruisers were all oil-fired, and although many people (even some very well-known railway historians) still think that the 'Jellicoe Specials' were transporting coal for the mighty 'Dreadnoughts', in reality, the railways were carrying coal fuel for the Merchant Navy, naval support vessels, and the smaller and older units of the Royal Navy (most of which did of course consume prodigious quantities of Welsh steam coal).

Although railwaymen were exempted from conscription when that measure was introduced, many men had been members of the pre-war reserve or volunteer forces, and they therefore joined the colours at the very start of World War I. Others

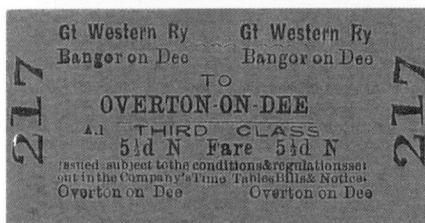
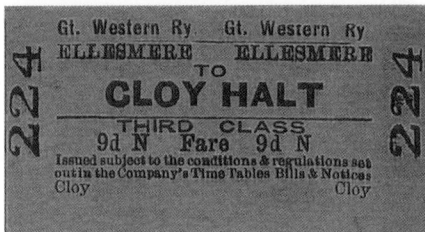
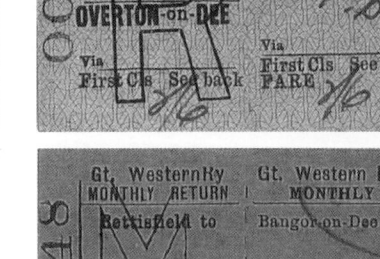
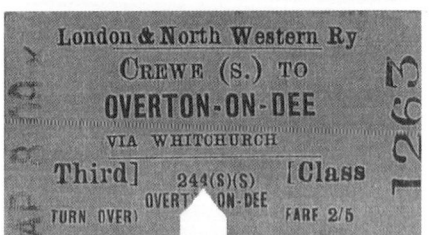
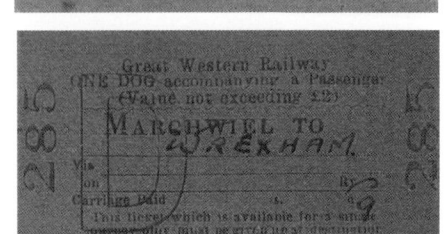
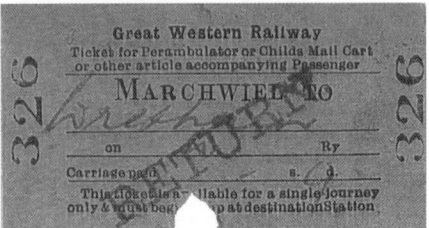

A selection of tickets from the pre-Nationalisation period.

volunteered, and for these reasons the Cambrian Railways (and other lines) were obliged to employ female staff as replacements for men serving in HM Forces.

Like all railways on the British mainland, the Cambrian and Wrexham & Ellesmere companies were placed under government control from the outbreak of war in 1914, and this period of supervision lasted until August 1921. In that same month, the passing of the 1921 Railways Act heralded the end of the old-time companies, which would henceforth be 'grouped' into four large undertakings. The Cambrian Railways became a constituent of the GWR in the early part of 1922, while on 1st July, 1922 the Wrexham & Ellesmere Railway was formally absorbed by the Great Western company.

In modern terms, the Wrexham & Ellesmere Railway had been a track and infrastructure company, whereas the Cambrian had acted as the 'train operating company' for the Wrexham & Ellesmere section; however, in 1922 the Grouping brought this situation to an end, and for the first time operation and infrastructure became unified under the enlarged GWR. On a footnote, it is worth mentioning that in 1921 the percentage dividend on Wrexham & Ellesmere shares was calculated as two per cent, while the Cambrian itself was in the unfortunate position of being unable to pay any dividend at all on its ordinary shares.

Changes and Improvements during the Great Western Period

The Great Western lost no time in implementing a programme of modest improvements on the Wrexham & Ellesmere branch. A new halt was, for instance, opened at Hightown on the outskirts of Wrexham in July 1923, while, in the years following the Grouping the GWR installed the electric train token in place of the earlier tablet system.

Until World War I, railway companies such as the GWR had enjoyed a virtual monopoly of land transport, and in these circumstances they were able to operate a large number of rural branch lines that were never more than marginally profitable. Some lines may have even lost money, but this situation was tolerated because of the 'system effect', whereby short, local lines could feed profitable traffic onto the main line network. In the changing economic conditions after World War I, the growth of road transport, rising wage bills and other factors made it increasingly difficult for lightly-used branch lines to survive, and the Great Western was obliged to seek a number of economies.

In the mid-1920s, the company carried out a thorough review of its entire branch line operations and, as a result, a programme of economies was put into effect. In a very few cases, it was reluctantly agreed that line closures would have to take place, but in general the GWR branch line review recommended the introduction of operating economics such as track rationalisation or staff cuts. In the latter context, the GWR effectively turned the intermediate stations at Overton-on-Dee, Bangor-on-Dee and Marchwiel into unstaffed halts. All station staff had been withdrawn by the mid-1930s, leaving just two signalmen on the staff establishment at each of these stations.

A typical example of a '517' class 0-4-2T, No. 534, with open cab. *R.W. Miller Collection*

There were many detail variations within the '517' class. This picture taken at Oswestry *c.*1925 shows No. 1423 with a round topped firebox and top feed. This engine was push-pull fitted. The bunker is most unusual, it was fitted sometime after 1924, withdrawal came in February 1930.

R.W. Miller Collection

DEVELOPMENTS DURING THE CAMBRIAN AND GWR PERIODS

In a further attempt to cut staff numbers and reduce costs on the Wrexham & Ellesmere line, the Great Western introduced mechanised methods of line maintenance, with reduced numbers of permanent way men using PW trolleys for routine inspection and maintenance work. In earlier days, work of this kind had been carried out by gangers who patrolled their sections of line on foot, but the introduction of the 'Motor Economic' system of track maintenance enabled just one mechanised Permanent Way gang to become responsible for the entire branch between Cambrian Junction (Ellesmere) and Wrexham Central station.

This system necessitated a degree of technical sophistication in that, in order that the petrol-engined motor trolley could safely work on the single line, the ganger responsible for the line was furnished with an Occupation Key system that worked in conjunction with the normal single line signalling system. When a key was withdrawn from its instrument, the PW gang gained occupation of the single line, and no trains could then enter the section of line concerned. To facilitate this mode of operation nine 'Key Boxes' were installed at regular intervals along the line, each box being equipped with its own instrument and telephone link to the appropriate signal box.

The branch permanent way gang were able to travel to the place at which their work would be taking place in a motorised trolley which, if necessary, was able to tow a trailer; in addition, the ganger was required to inspect the line regularly in a small inspection car.

In 1930 the junction arrangements at Ellesmere were further simplified when the signal box that had formerly stood beside the down side of the main line at Ellesmere East Junction was abolished; besides saving in maintenance costs, this track rationalisation also allowed a reduction in the number of signalmen at Ellesmere from six to three. On a footnote, it is interesting to note that a government ordnance siding had been installed on the site of the former West Junction, this facility being known as the Ellesmere 'Old Loop Siding'.

In the 1930s the single line between Ellesmere and Wrexham Central was worked in four sections as shown below:

Ellesmere Station to Overton-on-Dee	Electric token
Overton-on-Dee to Bangor-on-Dee	Electric token
Bangor-on-Dee to Marchwiel	Electric token
Marchwiel to Wrexham Central	Electric tablet

Operating the Line in the Great Western Era

Push-pull working was the usual method of operation for passenger trains during the Great Western era, with '517' class 0-4-2Ts being widely used on the Wrexham to Ellesmere auto-train services. Several different '517s' were stationed at Oswestry at various times for work on the Wrexham & Ellesmere route and other local branch lines. Among the engines known to have worked in the area during the 1920s and 1930s were Nos. 523, 574, 1423 and 1435. The passenger vehicles on the local routes at this time included Nos. 7026, 7028 and 7216; these were all former main line composite coaches that had been adapted for push-pull working.

Wrexham (Rhosddu) engine shed in Great Central days. In shed yard are Cambrian Railways 0-6-0 No. 79 on the left, a MS&LR 0-6-2T, and three WM&CQ Beyer, Peacock 0-6-2STs (including Nos. 403, 406). *R. M. Casserley Collection*

Cambrian Railways 0-6-0 No. 79 was built by the Vulcan Foundry in 1894 (Works No. 1446). It is shown here as GWR No. 882 outside the works at Oswestry; engines of this type worked local goods trains for many years. No. 882 was finally withdrawn in January 1935.
S.C. Jenkins/Lens of Sutton Collection

DEVELOPMENTS DURING THE CAMBRIAN AND GWR PERIODS 53

Wrexham & Ellesmere workings formed part of a pattern of operation in which individual train sets performed a variety of duties throughout the Shropshire and North Wales areas. Typical rosters, around 1930-32, involved engines and trailers based at both Oswestry and Croes Newydd (Wrexham), with trips from Wrexham to Chester, Chester to Llangollen or Corwen, Corwen to Wrexham and Gobowen to Oswestry, as well as trips on the Wrexham & Ellesmere and Llanfyllin branches.

In general, the Wrexham & Ellesmere branch train worked out from Oswestry to Ellesmere at the start of each day's operation, and returned empty stock from Ellesmere at 10.00 pm after the cessation of the branch train service. Single coaches were the norm on the Wrexham & Ellesmere route, and photographic evidence suggests that the locomotive was invariably coupled at the south (Ellesmere) end of the passenger vehicle.

The Collett '48XX' (later '14XX') class 0-4-2Ts were introduced in 1932 as replacements for the Armstrong '517' class 0-4-2Ts and other elderly GWR tank engines. The new 0-4-2T locomotives appeared in the Oswestry area during the 1930s, and these newly-built engines soon turned up on the Wrexham line. In 1932, Collett 0-4-2Ts Nos. 4812 and 4815 were both stationed at Oswestry, while sister engine No. 4810 was shedded at neighbouring Croes Newydd. By 1938, the Oswestry-based Collett 0-4-2Ts were Nos. 4815, 4832 and 4859.

The Wrexham & Ellesmere branch was classified as a 'Blue' route under the Great Western system of weight restrictions, all engines in the 'Yellow' and 'uncoloured' categories being permitted to work throughout from Wrexham to Ellesmere, while heavier 'blue' locomotives (except 2-8-0 classes) were allowed to run on the line subject to special speed restrictions and local prohibitions.

Although not strictly relevant to the Wrexham & Ellesmere line, it may be worth mentioning that the former Wrexham, Mold & Connah's Quay route was worked by former Great Central classes - particularly the Robinson 'C13' class 4-4-2Ts which worked most passenger services into and out of Wrexham Central. Other LNER types, including Robinson 'J11' class 0-6-0s and former Lancashire, Derbyshire & East Coast Railway 'J60' class 0-6-0Ts, could be seen on freight and shunting duties in and around Wrexham.

The LNER had its own motive power depot at Wrexham (Rhosddu) which was near, but entirely separate from, the Great Western sheds at Croes Newydd. The GWR and LNER routes were physically-linked at Wrexham, but there appears to have been little through running as far as engine workings were concerned, and Oswestry remained the principal shed for Wrexham & Ellesmere branch engines.

The train service provided in the late 1920s and early 1930s comprised around eight workings in each direction between Ellesmere and Wrexham, with an additional down trip on Saturdays only from Ellesmere at 1.30 pm.

In 1932, passenger operation began with the departure of the branch train from Oswestry at 8.07 am. This locomotive and auto-trailer formed the first down working from Ellesmere. Meanwhile, at 7.50 am, another engine and coach(es) had left Wrexham Central as an up service, and these two workings passed in the crossing loop at Overton-on-Dee at 8.15 am. The up and down services reached their destinations at 8.28 am and 8.41 am respectively. Thereafter, the train that had started its operations at the northern end of the line returned to Wrexham from Ellesmere at 8.50 am, while the Oswestry-based branch train formed the next up service from Wrexham to Ellesmere at 9.45 am.

The ensuing pattern of operation was relatively simple in that the train from Oswestry (a single auto-car, having third class accommodation only) shuttled backwards and forwards for the rest of the day, with down trips from Ellesmere to Wrexham at 10.30, 11.50 am, 2.42, 4.15, 5.45 and 7.25 pm. In the reverse direction, balancing up services left Wrexham Central at 11.07 am, 1.30, 3.30, 5.03, 6.40 and 9.00 pm. The last train of the day reached Ellesmere by 9.35 pm, after which, as mentioned earlier, the train returned to Oswestry for servicing and overnight stabling.

This basic timetable did not change in any appreciable way throughout the 1930s, apart from one or two minor alterations in times of arrival and departure. The one innovation, in the 1930s, concerned the opening of further halts, which were added at intervals during that decade. Cloy Halt, between Overton-on-Dee and Bangor-on-Dee, was opened on 30th June, 1932, while Elson Halt, near Ellesmere, was added on 8th February, 1937; a further halt was opened at Pickhill (near Marchwiel) on 30th May, 1938.

The summer 1939 train service was generally similar to its 1932 predecessor, with eight trains in each direction on weekdays and an extra down service on Saturdays. In the up direction, trains left Wrexham Central at 7.43, 9.45, 11.07 am, 1.30, 3.30, 5.03, 6.40 and 9.00 pm, while the corresponding down services departed from Ellesmere at 8.05, 8.50, 10.29 am, 12.00 noon, 2.40, 4.15, 5.45 and 7.25 pm.

As in 1932, two trains were needed to work the daily service, the single coach branch auto-train being used for most workings, while an additional Wrexham-based set formed a single out-and-back trip from Wrexham Central at 7.43 am. The normal branch auto-service was shown in GWR public timetables as a 'Rail Motor Car, one class only', though the Wrexham-based train had accommodation for first class travellers as well as third class ticket-holders.

There are indications that the first up and second down services may have been worked by a conventional non-corridor two-coach set (at least on occasions) though, at the same time, it is possible that a composite auto-trailer may have been rostered. Perhaps significantly, the 7.43 am up and 8.50 am down workings were *not* shown as 'rail motors' in the public timetables. These two Wrexham-based services were normally worked by the engine of the first freight working from Oswestry which reached Caia goods yard around 7.00 am.

Collection & Delivery Arrangements in the 1920s and 1930s

Like many other lines planned during the Victorian era, the Wrexham & Ellesmere branch was equipped with stations sited at regular intervals along the line, with uniform distances of about three miles between each station and goods yard. This generous distribution of stations was designed to complement a road transport system worked exclusively by horses, each station being seen as a convenient railhead for a group of villages and hamlets.

The years following the end of World War I saw a great upsurge in the road transport industry. The war itself had produced vast numbers of new, and improved road vehicles, and large numbers of these were sold to private owners in the 1920s. Many former servicemen used their gratuities to start 'one man' transport undertakings, and at a time when there were no restrictions or licensing controls on road goods vehicles, these 'cowboy' operators were able to undercut the railways in a relentless fight for traffic.

The railway companies responded in many ways, the new halts mentioned above being just one response to the threat posed by road transport. In an effort to combat competition on the goods front, the GWR itself became a large-scale user of motorised road transport, with railway-owned delivery vehicles being employed to provide road feeder services for the door-to-door collection and distribution of freight and parcels traffic. These comprehensive road services were designed to work in conjunction with the rail network and, in many instances, the Great Western was able to win back traffic from the private road hauliers.

The Great Western made use of its large fleet of motor vehicles in several ways. Most stations of moderate importance were served by cartage services within clearly defined geographical areas. In general, goods and parcels were collected or delivered free within these areas, though traders and residents on the outer fringes of urban areas were usually charged a small fee. In rural areas, certain stations were selected for development as 'country lorry centres', from which small fleets of road vehicles could be used to serve the surrounding area.

The company's road delivery services were so successful that the railway was prepared to undertake the transport of non-railborne traffic such as roadstone for local authorities, or feed stuffs for farmers and agricultural merchants. Household removals became a particular speciality, demountable road-rail containers being ideal for this class of traffic. Charges were based upon a fixed hourly rate for the lorry and driver, and the estimated time that would be needed to perform the whole removal operation. If necessary, expert packers could be supplied by the GWR in return for an extra charge, while for longer distances the containers could be forwarded by fast freight trains.

The 'country lorry services' worked on an entirely different basis. In this case, the motor vehicles assigned to particular services followed regular routes that took them well beyond the normal cartage areas. Outlying farms and villages were thereby linked to the railway system by regular collection and delivery services, every class of traffic being conveyed at reasonable rates. The country lorries served comparatively wide rural areas, and they were, to some extent, themselves in competition with traffic from smaller stations and goods depots (though as the delivery vehicles concerned were railway-owned, this did not greatly matter).

As far as the Wrexham & Ellesmere route is concerned, the development of these railway-operated road services was perhaps a mixed blessing. Although Ellesmere became a country lorry centre, Overton-on-Dee, Bangor-on-Dee and Marchwiel stations were not served by any of the railway delivery services, and this can only have been detrimental to traffic growth. As might be expected, Wrexham became an important cartage centre, and its vehicles served the northern end of the Wrexham & Ellesmere line as far south as Hightown Halt.

So long as the GWR and the other railway companies were allowed to maintain their own fleets of wholly-owned road vehicles this competition did not greatly matter, as the companies concerned were able to use road transport to combat the challenge from road transport operators - the main point being that trunk hauls still took place by rail, while customers were offered a door-to-door transport service for their goods and parcels.

In 1938 the GWR published a staff handbook known as the book of *Towns, Villages & Outlying Works*. This substantial 896-page volume was intended as an 'at a glance' guide to the collection and delivery arrangements at each destination served by the GWR, each town, village and hamlet being listed alphabetically. The book shows the mode of conveyance from the nearest Great Western station, together with the distance in miles and fractions from each railhead.

Examination of this interesting volume provides a somewhat pessimistic picture insofar as the Wrexham & Ellesmere route does not appear to have been particularly well served by the GWR. A glance at Table One *(below)* will reveal that, only at its extremities, was the line properly served by Great Western road delivery vehicles.

Table One

Goods & Parcels Delivery Arrangements on the Wrexham & Ellesmere Line, 1938

Name of Place	Distance from station	Delivery Arrangements
Ellesmere	n/a	Country lorry centre
Elson Halt	1 mile*	Lorry service from Ellesmere
Trench Halt	n/a	No arrangements
Overton-on-Dee	1 mile	Private carrier service
Cloy Halt	n/a	No delivery arrangements
Bangor-on-Dee	¾ mile	Private carrier service
Pickhill Halt	n/a	No delivery arrangements
Sesswick Halt	3 miles*	Private carrier from Bangor
Marchwiel	¼ mile	Private carrier service
Hightown Halt	1½ miles*	Cartage service from Wrexham
Wrexham Central	n/a	Railway cartage service

* Distance shown is from the nearest station served by road vehicles.

The paucity of collection and delivery services suggests that the Great Western was unwilling to develop this former Cambrian branch when the area was already being served by other, more important Great Western routes such as the Shrewsbury & Chester main line. The latter route had country lorry centres at Ruabon and Rossett, as well as the cartage services at Wrexham; another Great Western country lorry centre was established at Oswestry, on the Cambrian line from Whitchurch to Welshpool.

There was, in addition, an element of 'competition' from the LNER at Wrexham and the London Midland & Scottish Railway at Whitchurch and Malpas. At a time when all of the railways were fighting road competition, the 'Big Four' railway companies were loath to compete openly among themselves, and for this reason various pooling and zoning agreements were established whereby demarcation lines were set up around particular railheads; the area to

DEVELOPMENTS DURING THE CAMBRIAN AND GWR PERIODS 57

the east of Bangor-on-Dee, for instance, could be served from Malpas LMS station on that company's branch from Whitchurch, and it therefore made little sense for the GWR to provide a duplicate lorry service from Bangor-on-Dee.

Another important consideration was the fact that the Wrexham & Ellesmere line ran through a sparsely-populated district which would probably have been unable to sustain a comprehensive network of road feeder services even if the GWR had been willing to provide these facilities! In truth, the line had been built for 'political' rather than purely economic reasons, and with road transport posing an ever-greater threat to its viability, the future of this rural branch was already in some doubt.

Goods Trains & Traffic

One sphere of activity in which the line had shown some promise was in relation to private siding traffic. Successive editions of *The Railway Clearing House Handbook of Stations* show that these facilities were increased throughout the years in answer to the transport needs of brick works and other local industries. In 1910, for example, Elson brick works siding between Ellesmere and Bangor-on-Dee was already in use, while Kings Mill brick siding between Marchwiel and Wrexham was also in use from an early date. Five Fords agricultural siding near Marchwiel was brought into use around 1904, and the Cadbury Creamery siding near Pickhill Halt was added in the 1930s.

The 1938 edition of *The Railway Clearing House Handbook of Stations* reveals that there were six private sidings in use at that date. These are listed in Table Two (*overleaf*) which shows the various stations, halts and goods sidings *en route* from Ellesmere to Wrexham Central.

For completeness, the table also shows the range of facilities available at each location, the standard Railway Clearing House abbreviations such as 'P' for passenger and parcels station and 'G' for goods station being used as appropriate. These abbreviations have been modified slightly, and the various goods sidings have been placed in their geographical positions as far as possible. It should be noted that the presence of an 'H', 'C' or 'F' abbreviation indicates that the stations concerned were equipped with an end-loading dock, while 'L' shows that cattle pens were included among the station accommodation.

Ellesmere station in 1947 looking towards Oswestry with the goods yard in the foreground.
S. C. Jenkins Collection

This private owner wagon for H.E. Roberts, coal merchant at Overton-on-Dee, was a product of the Midland Railway Carriage & Wagon Co. Ltd in Birmingham. *Coutanche Collection*

DEVELOPMENTS DURING THE CAMBRIAN AND GWR PERIODS 59

Table Two

Stations, Sidings and Goods Depots on the Wrexham & Ellesmere Line, circa 1938

Station or Halt	Accommodation	Crane	Private Sidings, etc.
Ellesmere	G P F L H C	1 ton	'The Old Loop Siding' (out of use)
Elson Halt	P		Elson Siding (out of use)
Trench Halt	P		Trench Siding
Overton-on-Dee	G P F L H C	6 ton	
Cloy Halt	P		
Bangor-on-Dee	G P F L H C		
Pickhill Halt	P		Cadbury Brothers siding
Sesswick Halt	P		
Marchwiel	G P F L H C		Five Fords farm siding
Hightown Halt	P		Abenbury brick works siding
			Kings Mill brick works siding
Caia Goods Station	G L	1½ ton	
Wrexham Central	G P F L H C	5 ton	Cobden flour mill siding

G = Goods station. P = passenger station. L = livestock.
F = Furniture vans, road vehicles, machinery, etc.
H = Horse boxes & prize cattle vans. C = carriages & motor cars.

In addition to the above-mentioned sidings, Hightown siding, near Hightown Halt, and Marchwiel Ordnance Factory sidings were brought into use during World War II to cater for ammunition traffic and other vital commodities.

At the risk of stating the obvious, it may be worth adding that the goods rolling stock seen on the Wrexham & Ellesmere line reflected the types of traffic carried over the route, with wooden-bodied open wagons much in evidence throughout the line's existence. Such vehicles were used for both coal traffic and various general merchandise traffic - though in later years many kinds of non-coal traffic were conveyed in covered vans.

As far as can be ascertained, domestic coal was usually delivered to local stations in privately-owned colliery or traders' wagons, while Great Western opens were used for the conveyance of hay, straw, building materials, bricks, and other types of general goods traffic. Cattle were transported in standard GWR 'Mex' cattle wagons, while perishables were carried in a range of specialised GWR vehicles including refrigerated 'Mica Bs'. Milk traffic was conveyed from a CWS milk depot at Overton in glass-lined milk tank wagons.

The quantities of traffic carried over the Wrexham & Ellesmere line cannot easily be estimated. It is impossible, for example, to ascertain the amount of through traffic that would have passed over the route in any given year - though such traffic is unlikely to have been very significant. Traffic statistics are, on the other hand, available for each of the intermediate stations, and it can be confidently stated that the average amount of freight handled at each of the three stations during the early 1930s was no more than 3,700 tons per annum.

The various private sidings were not treated separately for normal accounting purposes, and the figures quoted above will therefore include at least some traffic from Five Fords farm siding (which was included with

Marchwiel's annual traffic returns). To add to the confusion, the sidings at the northernmost extremity of the line were included with Wrexham Central's traffic statistics. However, by adding the total quantity of goods traffic handled at Wrexham Central to the combined total for the three intermediate stations (and their respective private sidings) the following picture emerges for the period *circa* 1930-34:

Goods tonnage handled at Wrexham Central (& sidings)	approx. 20,000 tons
Goods tonnage for intermediate stations (& sidings)	approx. 12,000 tons
Combined total per annum for period under review	32,000 tons

Goods traffic was conveyed by two trains in each direction, the first of which left Ellesmere at 5.45 am and reached Wrexham (Caia goods depot) by 7.05 am, having called at the intermediate stations if required. A second down goods working left Ellesmere at 11.42 am and arrived in Wrexham at 1.51 pm after calling *en route* at Overton-on-Dee, Bangor-on-Dee and Marchwiel.

In the up direction, the first southbound goods service left Wrexham at 10.00 am and reached Ellesmere by 1.30 pm, while a second up train left Wrexham at 1.10 pm (Mondays only) or 2.15 pm (Mondays and Saturdays excepted).

The southbound goods workings called at the intermediate stations and most of the private sidings, and for this reason the up journeys took much longer to accomplish than corresponding journeys in the down direction. It should perhaps be mentioned that most of the private sidings between Wrexham and Ellesmere were connected to the running line by single turnouts that were facing in the direction of Ellesmere. The sidings in question were, therefore, served primarily by up trains - though (as we shall see) propelling movements from the nearest convenient station were also permitted.

World War II

On Sunday 3rd September, 1939 the people of Britain heard, on their 'wireless' sets, that the German Chancellor Herr Hitler had refused to withdraw his forces from, Poland and that, in consequence, this country was at war with Germany.

In reality, the British Government had been preparing for war for several weeks, and the mass evacuation of children from large cities such as London and Liverpool had already commenced. Air Raid Precautions or 'ARP' measures were well advanced, while on 1st September, 1939 the Government had taken control of the 'Big Four' railways and London Transport under the terms of the Emergency Powers (Defence) Act 1939.

Government 'experts' were initially concerned that the enemy would launch a series of so-called 'knock-out blows' against British cities, and many people expected that the skies would soon be black with Luftwaffe bombers; high explosive and poison gas attacks were thought to be imminent, and in anticipation of sudden air attack nightly black-out measures were strictly enforced.

With the railway system under state control, drastically reduced train services were immediately put into effect; the first official war timetable came into force on Monday 25th September, 1939, and as far as the Wrexham & Ellesmere line was concerned this entailed a loss of three passenger workings in each direction, leaving a minimal service of five up and five down trains between Wrexham and Ellesmere. In the up direction, trains left Wrexham at 7.43, 11.07 am, 3.30, 5.03 and 6.40 pm, with balancing down services from Ellesmere at 8.50, 10.29 am, 12.00 noon, 4.15 and 5.45 pm.

Happily, the expected 'knock-out blow' was never delivered, and in retrospect it is now thought unlikely that Adolf Hitler ever seriously intended to invade Britain. Although military action was clearly taking place at sea, and in other theatres of war, the Home Front was so quiet that people spoke derisively of a 'Phoney War'. Local train services were gradually reinstated, and by February 1940 the Wrexham & Ellesmere branch was being served by a slightly improved service of six trains each way on weekdays rising to seven up and seven down workings on Saturdays.

By the spring of 1940 up trains were leaving Wrexham at 7.43, 9.45, 11.07 am, 3.30, 5.03, 6.40 and 9.00 pm (SO). In the down direction, northbound workings departed from Ellesmere at 8.05, 8.50, 10.29 am, 12.00 noon (Saturdays excepted), 12.15 (SO), 4.15, 5.45 and 7.25 pm (SO).

On 10th May, 1940 the German forces finally struck in Western Europe, and the massive French army collapsed within a matter of days; by June 1940 the British army had been withdrawn from the beaches of Dunkirk, and Britain itself began to prepare for an enemy invasion.

Perhaps surprisingly, the thought that Britain might actually *lose* the war does not seem to have arisen, and although the whole power of the German Luftwaffe was soon being directed against industrial cities such as Liverpool and Birmingham, the British Government was already preparing the first tentative plans for a cross-Channel counter-attack that would eventually liberate Europe.

It was clear that huge amounts of armaments and other vital equipment would be necessary before the liberation of Europe could take place, and Britain was soon producing enormous quantities of bombs, shells and other explosives. With armaments factories working night and day on a three-shift system, these massive stocks of arms and ammunition needed special storage facilities, and a network of purpose-built Central Ammunition Depots was rapidly set up. Emergency munitions factories were also established, one such factory being set up near Marchwiel, on the Wrexham & Ellesmere line.

Most of the large wartime ordnance depots and factories were served by rail - rail transport being regarded as an essential feature of the national war effort. At Marchwiel, the Royal Ordnance Factory was linked to the Wrexham & Ellesmere branch by a siding connection, while the factory itself was equipped with around nine miles of internal sidings. This new facility was worked under the terms of a private siding agreement signed on 12th August, 1941.

The Marchwiel site was important enough to justify the provision of a new signal cabin known as Marchwiel Factory Signal Box. This controlled the connections to the ordnance factory sidings, and the box also formed an additional block post, the single line between Wrexham and Ellesmere being worked as follows:

From	To	Signal Box	Worked by
Ellesmere	Overton-on-Dee	Ellesmere Station	Electric token
Overton-on-Dee	Bangor-on-Dee	Overton-on-Dee	Electric token
Bangor-on-Dee	Marchwiel Factory	Bangor-on-Dee	Electric tablet
Marchwiel Factory	Marchwiel	Marchwiel Factory	Electric token
Marchwiel	Wrexham Central	Marchwiel	Electric tablet
		Wrexham Central	–

An auxiliary token instrument was provided in connection with the Marchwiel Factory to Marchwiel station token circuit, the instrument being located in a shelter at the Marchwiel station end of the up and down loops.

As the war effort got into its full stride, various other private sidings on the Wrexham & Ellesmere branch were pressed into use by the Ministry of Supply or other wartime organisations. Five Fords Siding, for instance, was brought under the control of the Ministry of Supply, while Elson Siding, which had fallen out of use in the 1930s, was brought back into commission in connection with the establishment of a military supply and storage depot on a site adjacent to the railway near Elson Halt. Meanwhile, at nearby Ellesmere, the Old Loop Siding on the site of Ellesmere West Junction was reinstated for government traffic.

Most of the private sidings on the Wrexham & Ellesmere line were eventually pressed into use for the war effort, while the branch itself was increasingly used for the movement of munitions and other vital equipment. This wartime role was primarily concerned with freight transport, and there was less pressure on the line's modest passenger services. Indeed, the route was carrying so little originating passenger traffic that on 8th June, 1940, regular passenger services between Wrexham and Ellesmere were suspended for the duration of the war. Passengers were directed to the Crosville Motor Services bus service between the two points.

Security considerations may have been a factor in the decision to withdraw passenger services from the line, though in retrospect it is perhaps more likely that the decision to close the line was taken so that construction work at the Marchwiel site could take priority.

There were in fact *two* factories at Marchwiel, the first of which - known as No. 35 Royal Ordnance Factory - was built by Paulings & Company, while the neighbouring No. 36 Royal Ordnance Factory was constructed by Messrs Holland & Hannen and Cubitts. The first parts of the factory were in use by November 1940, major construction work having proceeded apace throughout the previous few months.

The construction phase of the Marchwiel Factories (subsequently merged to become No. 35 ROF) was, by any definition, a major civil engineering project, and large numbers of building workers travelled daily by rail to the site. Initially, it is believed that workers' specials ran to and from Sesswick Halt, from where motor transport was laid on to take them into the ROF site. Later, however, the trains ran only as far as Wrexham, and fleets of buses then ferried the workers to and from the factory - around 200 road vehicles being needed for this purpose.

The Marchwiel ROF was at its peak by 1944 - by which time the internal railway system had grown to a network of about nine miles, with a four mile 'main line' linking the various spurs and sidings. Passing loops were provided at strategic intervals, and there was a full-size station near the main line connection at the south-eastern extremity of the site. Elsewhere, small 'stations' were dotted around the site, while sidings and branch lines ran off to serve a variety of factory buildings and storage bunkers.

Former engine driver Jack Wilkinson, who regularly worked the Wrexham & Ellesmere branch during the war years, cannot remember the main internal station ever being used by passenger trains, though others recall the use of the internal ROF system for the movement of civilian workers once they had arrived at the factory by bus from Wrexham.

The factory itself seems to have specialised in the manufacture of propellants, though such details were never made public at the time, and it is possible that a whole range of explosives was produced on the site.

The wartime freight timetable consisted of a basic service of three trains in each direction, with only minor variations in terms of arrival and departure times. By 1944, the first down working (which had earlier worked out from Oswestry) was leaving Ellesmere at 6.20 am; it reached Wrexham at 7.30 am, and returned to Ellesmere at 8.10 am. A second train departed from Ellesmere at 12.15 pm and arrived at Wrexham by 2.40 pm, while a third service left Ellesmere at 3.45 pm and reached Wrexham at 5.20 pm. These two trains were balanced by up departures from Wrexham at 3.30 and 5.50 pm respectively.

There were, in addition, shorter distance trips from Ellesmere to Overton at 9.15 am (return 10.45 am), and from Wrexham to Marchwiel at 8.10 am. Jack Wilkinson recalled that, at various times, the Overton service ran through to Cadbury's siding at Pickhill and then on to Caia goods yard and Wrexham.

The Wrexham & Ellesmere branch was, by 1944, working at full stretch to serve the various wartime establishments *en route* to Wrexham. These included Elson military storage siding, a similar supply depot beside Overton-on-Dee station, Marchwiel Royal Ordnance Factory, and a new siding that had been installed at Hightown to serve a shadow aircraft production factory. There were, in addition, a number of other establishments in the area served by the railway including a large American Army transit camp and hospital at Penley, near Overton-on-Dee, and an RAF aerodrome at Barras, to the north-west of Wrexham.

At its peak, around June 1944, the Penley camp housed up to 2,000 American soldiers, while RAF Wrexham was used as a training site by 21 Group, Flying Training Command. It was serving as a satellite aerodrome for RAF Calveley in June 1944 and, as such, its aircraft allocation would have been mainly twin-engined Airspeed Oxford trainers.

These diverse establishments gave rise to many special trains during the war years - the period around June and July 1944 being particularly busy in connection with the D-Day invasion of Europe. The Allied forces anticipated large numbers of casualties in the first few days of the D-Day landings and preparations were made for the rapid evacuation of wounded men, certain sites being adapted for use as emergency hospitals. One such hospital was created at Penley Hall, the idea being that ambulance trains would be sent direct to Overton-on-Dee for unloading.

In practice, the numbers of casualties resulting from the D-Day operation were less than expected, and many of the emergency hospitals were never fully used for their original purpose. Nevertheless, local enginemen clearly recall one or two ambulance trains working through to Overton-on-Dee both before and after D-Day on 6th June, 1944 - the earlier trips being useful test runs for the 'real thing' once the invasion force had landed in Europe.

Former driver Ken Southern remembered one such special working in the period *before* D-Day, when he was working on the line as a young fireman. On this occasion a long train of passenger vehicles had been collected at Whitchurch, and he naturally assumed that it contained wounded soldiers. On reaching Overton-on-Dee the train crew asked an American military policemen or 'snow drop' (so-called because of their white helmets) what had happened to 'that lot behind'; the policeman merely smiled and said, 'Wait till you see them'. At that juncture the passengers started to disembark, and within minutes the lengthy platforms at Overton-on-Dee station were thronged with a seething mass of highly-pregnant young women!

On another occasion, Jack Wilkinson recalled taking two light engines to Whitchurch, where an ambulance train had arrived from the Southern Railway. The GWR locomotives then worked the special on to Overton-on-Dee, where the casualties were unloaded and taken to Penley and Halston Hall hospitals by road transport (he also recalled a similar emergency hospital at Oatley Hall, just outside Ellesmere).

The engines used on the Wrexham & Ellesmere route during World War II included the usual GWR pannier tank classes, notably '74XX' class 0-6-0PTs Nos. 7405, 7410 and 7434, together with one or two large prairie tanks, such as '81XX' class 2-6-2T No. 8103. The latter engine seems to have been used on a regular basis during the war years - presumably because of the heavy traffic that was then being carried over the line. No. 8103 was virtually a new engine, having been built in November 1938 as a member of the 10-strong '81XX' sub-class of large prairies; it was allocated to Stourbridge for a few years, but subsequently moved to Oswestry, where it remained until the early 1950s.

Tender engines were sometimes used on through specials, with '2251' class 0-6-0s, 'Dean Goods' 0-6-0s and 'Dukedog' class 4-4-0s putting in at least sporadic appearances. The largest engine seen on the line during the war years is believed to have been a former Great Eastern Railway 'B12' class 4-6-0, which is said to have worked a US Army hospital train through to Overton-on-Dee in 1944.

The war in Europe ended in May 1945, and Japan surrendered in the following August, but branch passenger services were not restored until May 1946, when a push-pull service of eight up and eight down workings was re-introduced between Wrexham and Ellesmere. Further details of these post-war services will be given in *Chapter Six*.

Passenger timetable, July 1947.

Chapter Four

The Stations and Route from Ellesmere to Sesswick

Having examined the history of the Wrexham & Ellesmere branch from its inception until World War II, it would now be convenient to study the route of this Cambrian Railways branch in greater detail, and this and the following chapter will therefore take readers on an imaginary guided tour of the line from Ellesmere to Wrexham Central. The topographical details in this section will be correct for the later GWR and early British Railways periods, while the datum point for the calculation of distances will be Ellesmere station. (For the purposes of this study, northbound services will be regarded as 'down' workings.)

Ellesmere

Ellesmere, the junction for branch services to Wrexham, was opened as part of the Oswestry, Ellesmere & Whitchurch line on 27th July, 1864. Its station buildings were large and impressive, the main block, on the down side, being a two-storey brick structure with gabled cross wings which faced the station approach, and a projecting bay window on the platform frontage. There was a platform canopy with graceful iron supports, and the upper floor windows were arched in the Italianate style.

Interestingly, the style of architecture adopted at Ellesmere was very similar to that employed elsewhere on the Cambrian and its constituents during the 1860s; Llanidloes, for example, was built to more or less the same plan, while nearby Oswestry boasted a much larger station building in the same basic style.

The track layout here consisted of a 1,158 ft crossing loop with sidings on both sides. The station was orientated on an east-to-west alignment, Ellesmere itself being to the south-east of the railway. Wrexham & Ellesmere trains ran into the station from the west, the junction being facing to down trains travelling in the direction of Oswestry. Elson Road was carried over the railway on a single-span brick bridge to the west of the platforms, while another road overbridge carried Grange Road across the line at the east end of the station.

There were no branch bays and, for this reason, Wrexham branch trains arrived in the main up platform and departed from the down side. When it was necessary for incoming branch trains to make connections with up main line workings, there was an arrangement whereby both trains could use the up platform. In such cases the up main line service was drawn forward towards the up starting signal until its rearmost vehicle was clear of the up inner home signal; the branch train was then allowed to enter the platform provided it was piloted from the up branch intermediate home signal by a competent shunter or guard.

Ellesmere's goods handling facilities were laid out on a relatively lavish scale. The goods yard was situated on the south or down side of the running lines, and it included a goods shed, coal sidings, cattle pens and a six ton fixed hand crane. Additional siding facilities were provided on the up side, these being

65

Ellesmere station. *Reproduced from the 25", 1909 Ordnance Survey Map*

entered via a siding connection that was trailing to up trains. Until the 1930s Ellesmere had two signal boxes, known as Ellesmere and Ellesmere Junction, in 1930, however, the Junction box was closed and its block instruments were transferred to the station box, which then had no less than five instruments. The surviving cabin was sited to the east of the platform on the up side. It was of brick and timber construction, with a gable roof.

Other features of interest at Ellesmere included a lattice girder footbridge between the up and down platforms, a weigh-house and the usual assortment of permanent way huts and sheds. Passenger facilities on the up side were confined to a small waiting room, with a low-pitched, slated roof. This small structure had brick side and end walls, and a timber facade. At night, the platforms were lit by gas.

A locomotive turntable with a diameter of 50 ft enabled tender engines to be turned to face the right direction before each journey; this facility was situated at the Whitchurch end of the station, on the up side of the running lines.

Ellesmere station provided employment for about 18-20 people. In the late 1920s, for example, the staffing establishment consisted of one class two station master, two booking clerks, two goods clerks, four porters, one goods checker, one goods shunter, two goods porters, two motor drivers and six signalmen. By the mid-1930s, however, modest staffing cuts had been put into effect, and by 1934-35 the staff establishment at Ellesmere was as follows:

Grade	No.	Classification
Station Master	1	Class Two
Booking Clerk	1	Class Four
Booking Clerk	1	Class Five
Goods Clerks	2	Class Five
Porters	2	Grade Two
Lad Porter	1	Junior
Goods Checker	1	-
Goods Porter	1	-
Goods Shunter	1	Class Four
Motor Driver	1	-
Goods Carter	1	-
Signalmen	3	Class Four
Total	16	

Ellesmere station was the scene of a minor derailment on Sunday 6th November, 1887, when a down mail train from Whitchurch to Oswestry was thrown off the line as it entered the station. This incident allegedly occurred through the negligence of porter John Humphrey, who was supposed to have operated a point lever incorrectly (there was no signal box at that time). Although there were strong indications that the derailment could have been caused by the poor condition of the trackwork in and around Ellesmere station, the Cambrian Railways management decided to place all the blame on the unfortunate porter, and he was dismissed from the company's service.

The matter could well have ended with John Humphrey's dismissal, but local opinion was suddenly aroused, and a petition was organised in support of the porter; moreover, the then station master, Mr John Hood, made it known that

Ellesmere station looking east towards Whitchurch during the BR era. The substantial red brick station buildings incorporated a variety of facilities including domestic accommodation for the local station master, and offices formerly used by the Wrexham & Ellesmere Railway Company.
S.C. Jenkins/Lens of Sutton Collection

The GWR station nameboard at Ellesmere, depicting the stations on the branch to Wrexham.
John White

he supported the sacked employee and (perhaps unwisely) he signed the petition. This inevitably brought him into conflict with the railway company, with the result that he was himself subjected to victimisation.

The dispute eventually reached the House of Commons, by which time the Cambrian Railways Company had itself been severely criticised for making its employees work long shifts for sustained periods - with obvious implications in terms of public safety. John Hood was forced to leave the railway, but happily he received generous compensation, and continued to live in Ellesmere as a successful and prosperous local citizen.

John Hood's immediate successors included Richard Gough, who served as station master at Ellesmere around the turn of the century, and John Chilson, who was in charge of the station in the years before World War I. The next station master was George Morgan, who was at Ellesmere by 1913, and remained at the station for many years thereafter.

A later station master was Mr J.W. Hobbs, who had also served at Bangor-on-Dee and other former Cambrian stations. When Mr Hobbs retired in 1946, *The Great Western Railway Magazine* printed the following notes on his career:

> Mr J.W. Hobbs, retiring from the post of station master, Ellesmere, after 46 years' service, has always found time for taking part in many social activities when his day's railway work is done. His wide interests have ranged from service on urban and parish councils to appearances on the amateur stage, at musical recitals and on the sports field. He has also devoted much of his leisure to church work, and was co-founder of a Sunday school at Fenn's Bank in 1913, and became a licensed lay reader in 1931. A native of Manchester, Mr Hobbs joined the Cambrian Railways in 1900 at Fenn's Bank, and after various experience in North Wales was appointed station master at Bangor-on-Dee eleven years later. Promoted to Towyn, he was transferred to Ellesmere in 1935.

Those employed at Ellesmere station during the British Railways era around 1960 included porter P.T. Walker, shunter F.J. Lloyd, signalman J.S. Mills, ganger R.V. Martin, lengthman C.G. Milburn and sub-ganger H. Humphreys.

The traffic handled at Ellesmere included coal, building materials, cattle, agricultural produce and road stone. Domestic coal was purchased, in bulk by local coal merchants such as Thomas Chetwood, who rented a coal wharf in the goods yard and was described in a 1900 trade directory as a 'coal, coke and lime' dealer; the business was later carried on by Ellis Chetwood, who was presumably the son of Thomas.

Other Ellesmere coal merchants in the years before World War I included Walter Nunnerley and J.F. Billington. The latter firm seems to have been a somewhat larger undertaking than most local coal merchants; Billingtons had coal wharves at Whitchurch, Bangor-on-Dee, Overton-on-Dee and other nearby stations, and they continued to trade in the area for many years.

Cattle traffic was also of considerable importance at Ellesmere, a busy cattle market being conveniently sited alongside the goods yard on the south side of the railway, with direct access from one of the sidings.

Ellesmere served as the economic centre of a large rural hinterland and, perhaps for this reason, the station was chosen by the GWR as one of a number of 'country lorry centres' from which smaller villages and hamlets could be

Collett '14XX' class 0-4-2T No. 1428 at Ellesmere, with a Wrexham working on 13th September, 1952.
C.H.A. Townley

Collett '2251' class 0-6-0 No. 3205 (now preserved) pauses at Ellesmere with a down main line working. Note the spacious station gardens to the right of the locomotive. In the distance, an unidentified '43XX' class mogul shunts the goods yard.
E.T. Gill

THE STATIONS AND ROUTE FROM ELLESMERE TO SESSWICK

A Collett '14XX' class 0-4-2T and train under the road bridge at the west end of Ellesmere station with the Wrexham auto-train. *John Tims*

Great Western mogul No. 7306 enters Ellesmere station with an up main line service, while Collett 0-6-0 No. 3205 occupies the down platform road. Baskets of pigeons and a new tyre await collection on the up platform. *E.T. Gill*

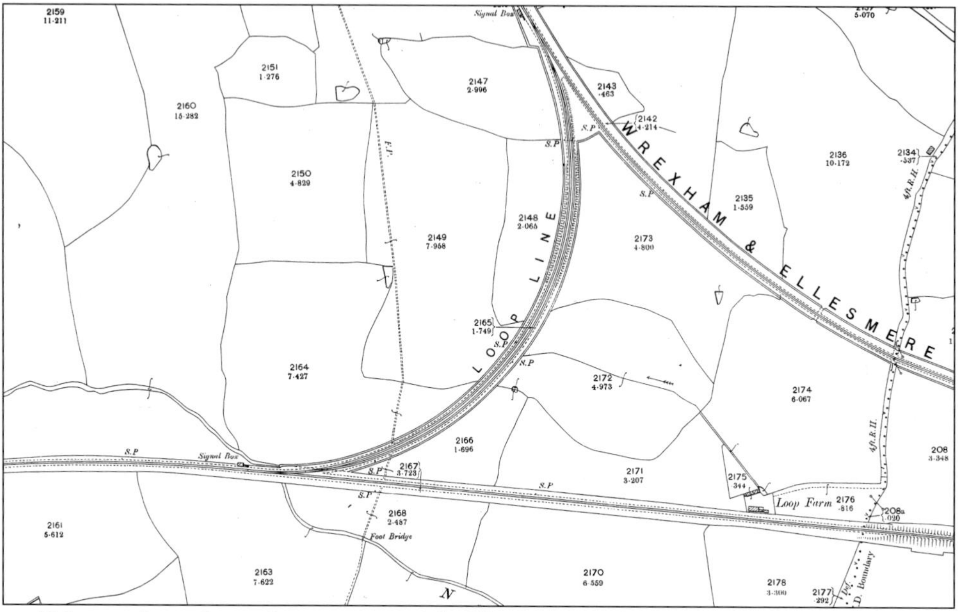

This map shows the north to west arm of the Ellesmere triangle still *in situ*. Note 'Loop Farm' beside the Oswestry-Whitchurch main line. *Reproduced from the 25", 1909 Ordnance Survey Map*

Ellesmere triangle, with the north to west link now removed and the Old Loop Siding now in place. *Reproduced from the 6", 1929 Ordnance Survey Map*

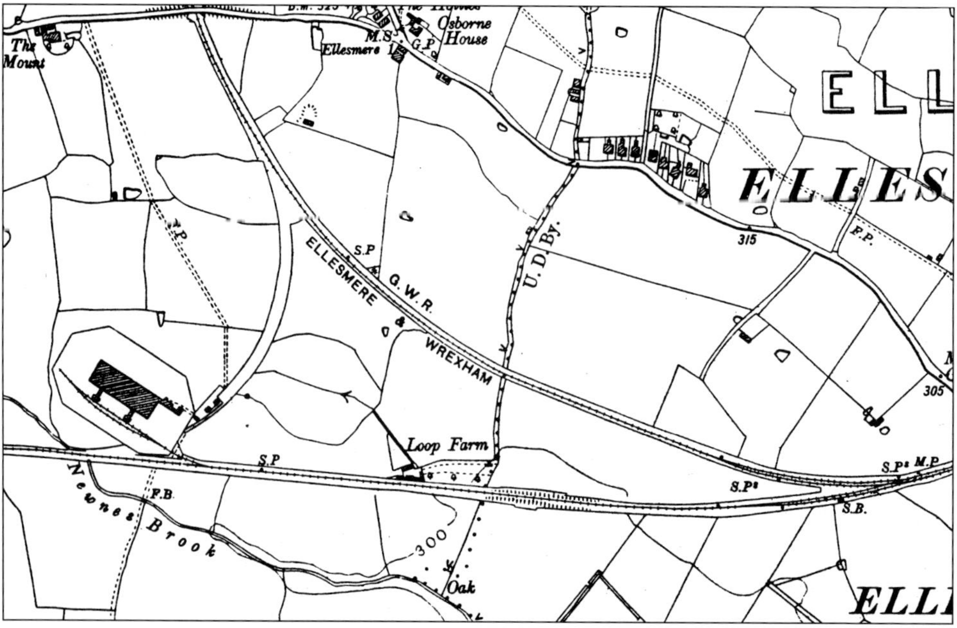

served by railway-owned road delivery vehicles. These vehicles collected or delivered goods and parcels to and from places such as Hordley (four miles from the station), Elson (one mile) and Colemere (three miles). In addition to this country lorry service, the GWR also provided a free collection and delivery service for traders and residents who lived within the confines of Ellesmere itself.

Ellesmere 'Old Loop Siding'

There was also, at various times, a traffic in munitions to and from the 'Old Loop Siding', and it would be convenient to add some further details here. The north-to-west arm of the Ellesmere triangle had been a controversial line from the very start, in that the residents of Ellesmere feared that it would be used to divert trains from Wrexham to Oswestry without stopping at the station. In fact, the north-to-west loop carried very little traffic of any kind, and it was more or less out of use by 1903. The loop was reopened around 1905, but it was then closed for a second, and final time; the trackwork and signals were removed, leaving only the formation, which soon became known as 'The Old Loop'.

At or about the end of World War I, the War Department erected a magazine at the south end of the former loop line, and this became known as 'The Old Loop Siding'. It was entered from the direction of Ellesmere by a facing connection from the single line, and the 1929 six inch OS map reveals that two lines were available within the magazine. The magazine siding extended north-westwards from the running line, and for this reason it did not follow the original alignment of the Old Loop (which diverged north-eastwards from the main line). The siding connection was, nevertheless, roughly on the site of the abandoned West Junction, the link to the running line being worked from a ground frame.

The 'Old Loop Siding' was out of use by the 1930s, and it is not listed in the 1938 *Railway Clearing House Handbook of Stations*. A connection to the magazine was restored during World War II, and instructions for working the siding were given in the 1943 Appendix to the Working Timetable. The siding was, by the end of World War II, sometimes referred to as 'Ellesmere Dump Siding'.

Leaving Ellesmere, Wrexham trains proceeded westwards for a short distance before diverging sharply rightwards onto the Wrexham & Ellesmere branch at Cambrian Junction, which was just 11 chains beyond Ellesmere passenger station. Taking up a northerly heading, the route began to climb towards Elson Halt on a 1 in 277 rising gradient.

Having turned through a full 90 degrees turn, Wrexham trains passed the long-abandoned north-to-west arm of the Ellesmere triangle which converged from the left at Ellesmere North Junction (61 chains from Ellesmere). There was at one time a signal box on the down side of the line, but this was abolished when the western arm of the triangle was abandoned.

Elson Halt, looking north (*above*), and south (*below*), in 1961. The platform here was only 75 ft long. Most of the halts on the Wrexham & Ellesmere were on the west side of the line, which ensured that they were on the driver's side of the train when the engine was in its usual position at the south end of the auto-car. *(Both) John M. Strange*

Elson Halt

The railway then passed beneath a minor road bridge, which was followed, in quick succession, by an overbridge carrying the B5068 across the line. On 8th February, 1937 the Great Western opened a small stopping place known as Elson Halt at a point 1 mile 12 chains from Ellesmere. This consisted of a short platform on the down side with a waiting shelter for intending passengers. The new halt was about a quarter of a mile to the north of Elson goods siding - the latter facility being a dead-end siding on the east side of the line that was entered via a connection which was facing to down trains.

The passenger platform, which was only 75 ft long, was of earth and timber construction, and the diminutive passenger shelter was formed of blackened timber. Public access was arranged via steps and a sloping ramp from the adjacent road overbridge. The latter structure was faced with courses of 'snecked' (or interrupted) stonework and, like all of the road overbridges *en route* to Wrexham, it had been built to accommodate a double line of rails. The only other facilities on the passenger platform were a nameboard and a single gas lamp.

For administrative purposes Elson Halt was under the control of the Ellesmere station master, and that official was expected to visit the halt from time to time in order to ensure that the premises were in a proper condition. Passengers joining their trains at the halt obtained their tickets from the guards, who were issued with supplies of the necessary Bell Punch-type vertical tickets.

Elson Siding

Elson Siding, which pre-dated the halt by many years, was shown in the 1910 *Railway Clearing House Handbook of Stations* as a brick works siding. The siding points were worked from a ground frame sited 71 chains from Ellesmere, which was locked by the electric train token for the Ellesmere to Overton-on-Dee single line section. The siding was served by up goods trains or by special pilot trips from Ellesmere.

When worked by pilot trips, trains of up to 16 goods vehicles were propelled along the line from Ellesmere on the outwards journey, with the brake van leading and the engine at the rear. During these operations the guard kept a sharp lookout for people who might otherwise have been unaware of the approach of the train. A white light was displayed on the leading vehicle after dark or during periods of fog or falling snow. In the reverse direction, up workings left the siding facing the 'right' direction with the locomotive leading in conventional fashion, though on the return journey the driver was warned that the line should be considered clear only as far as the Ellesmere up branch home signal.

An internal Great Western document reveals that Elson Siding was disconnected and out of use in the 1930s, but, like the neighbouring 'Old Loop Siding', it was reinstated during World War II to serve an army supply depot. Jack Wilkinson, who worked on the branch during the war years, remembered

Trench Halt looking north on 8th September, 1962. *C.C. Green/John M. Strange Collection*

Trench Halt viewed from the 1.30 pm service from Wrexham Central on 1st May, 1962. The platform here was a mere 45 ft long! *John White*

that the Elson site was used as 'a store for the military' dealing with 'various items too many to recall' including 'uniform clothing, bedding, hospital utensils, footwear, cycles, knives, forks, spoons' and numerous other types of equipment that would be needed by the army.

The Elson depot remained operative after the war as a supply centre; Jack Wilkinson suggested that as camps were closed at the end of hostilities much of their furnishings and equipment was sent to stores such as Elson for scrapping or reissue. Most of this traffic was sent to Elson in vans which were tripped from Ellesmere 'between trains in the mornings and afternoons'. Mr Wilkinson recalled that, in his experience, this traffic was usually taken to Overton-on-Dee station and then worked back towards Elson Halt so that the engine could shunt incoming vehicles into the siding.

Trench Halt and Siding

Leaving Elson Halt, down trains continued northwards through pleasant rural surroundings as the single line dropped towards the Dee Valley on gradients as steep as 1 in 84 and 1 in 85. At 1 mile 63 chains, the railway crossed a viaduct with a length of 80 yds.

Trench Halt, the next stopping place (2 miles 51 chains from Ellesmere), was opened by the Cambrian Railways in December 1914 to serve the inhabitants of nearby Trench and Upper Trench. Like other stations and halts on the Wrexham & Ellesmere branch, it was closed to passenger traffic on 8th June, 1940 and re-opened after the war in 1946.

Its facilities consisted of an utterly basic platform on the up side, with a rudimentary timber and corrugated iron shelter that provided scant comfort for the occasional traveller. The A528 road from Ellesmere to Wrexham crossed the line on a brick and girder bridge at the north end of the platform, access from the road being by means of a sloping cinder pathway. For administrative purposes Trench Halt was, like Elson, under the control of the Ellesmere station master.

Like nearby Elson Halt, Trench Halt was at one time the site of a private goods siding, though in this instance the siding had a very short life. A private siding agreement was made on 21st April, 1938, and the siding was listed in the 1938 *Railway Clearing House Handbook of Stations*; the GWR *Register of Private Sidings* shows, however, that Trench Siding was closed in 1941 - possibly because the traffic that had been handled there could more conveniently be dealt with at the neighbouring Elson Siding.

From Trench Halt, the single line ran due northwards, passing beneath another minor road bridge and then continuing across open farmland to the next station at Overton-on-Dee (4 miles 15 chains). The invisible boundary between England and Wales was sited a little to the north of Trench Halt, Trench itself being in Wales though the halt was situated on the English side of the border!

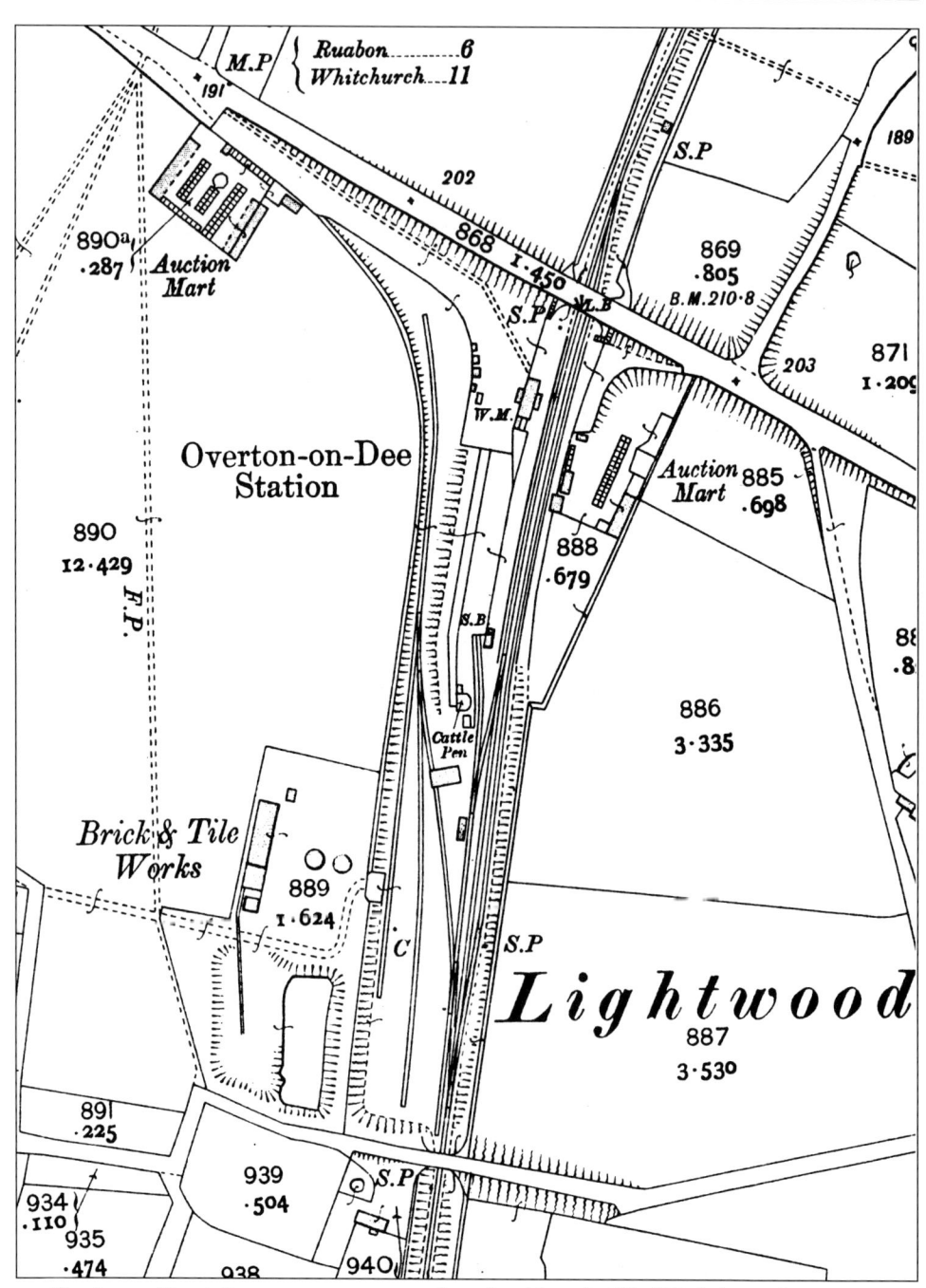

Overton-on-Dee station.   *Reproduced from the 25", 1909 Ordnance Survey Map*

Overton-on-Dee

Overton-on-Dee was a crossing station with up and down platforms, the main station buildings being on the down side. A road overbridge carried the A539 motor road across the line at the northern end of the platforms, and there was a typical Cambrian Railways gabled signal box at the south end of the down platform.

The goods yard, which contained a full range of facilities for coal, livestock and general merchandise traffic, was on the down side; a six ton fixed hand crane was available for use when heavy loads were transferred between road and rail traffic, and end-loading facilities were provided for vehicular traffic. The station was aligned from north to south, and its crossing loop had a length of 675 ft. An overall 10 mph speed restriction applied to trains travelling through the station in either direction.

The main station building was a timber-framed, weather-boarded structure with a gable roof. Internally it contained booking office and waiting room facilities, together with toilets for both sexes; the gentlemen's urinal occupied a small extension at the south end of the building. There was a small canopy, beneath which double doors gave access to the interior of the station. In later years at least this simple wooden structure was adorned in a traditional brown and cream colour scheme, brown being applied below waist height and around the windows - the frames of which were painted white.

The station building was roofed with Welsh slate and decorative terra-cotta ridge tiles, and its interior was finished with lath and plaster work. On a footnote, it is interesting to note that a similar design of cheaply-built, but attractive wooden station building was adopted on the Furness Railway during the 1890s - typical examples being erected at Eskmeals, Silecroft and Seascale. It is believed that the Wrexham & Ellesmere stations were designed by A.H. Aslett, and in this context it may not be entirely coincidental that his uncle, Alfred Aslett, became General Manager of the Furness Railway in 1895, having left the service of the Cambrian company to take up this new appointment.

The up platform was equipped with a small wooden waiting shelter with a sloping roof and slightly-arched windows. Both platforms were lit by simple oil lamps, and fenced with pale-and-space fencing. The station was signalled with home, starting and distant signals in each direction.

In earlier days Overton-on-Dee had been considered, important enough to have its own station master, but by the 1920s the staffing establishment had been cut down to just three men, including one grade one porter and two class five signalmen. In the early 1930s the porter's post was up-graded to a working foreman, but within a few years this post was deleted altogether and the station was then staffed by just two signalmen.

Those employed at Overton-on-Dee station in later years included signalmen S. Lancashire, Bill Speakman and Gwillam Roberts. Curiously, local people have suggested that the station was, at least on occasions, staffed; Mrs Sid Barclay, for example, mentioned that a Mr Evans was in charge of the station during World War II. She travelled regularly to and from Wrexham Grammar School from 1942 until 1947, and although for much of that time, the train service was worked by a

The south end of Overton-on-Dee station in August 1962. Note the cattle dock to the left. Ex-GWR 0-6-0 pannier tank No. 3789 stands in the platform with a goods train. It has just been passed by a Wrexham-bound passenger train (just visible at the far end of the station).

Overton-on-Dee signal box viewed from the 1.30 pm service from Wrexham on 1st May, 1962.
John White

THE STATIONS AND ROUTE FROM ELLESMERE TO SESSWICK 81

The goods yard and modest goods shed at Overton-on-Dee, looking towards Ellesmere, 8th September, 1962. *C.C. Green/John M. Strange Collection*

This view north along the platforms in 1961 clearly shows the station buildings.

John M. Strange

A Wrexham train at Overton-on-Dee, seen from the road overbridge which carried the Ruabon-Whitchurch (A539) road over the railway.

Collett '14XX' 0-4-2T and auto-car arrive at Overton-on-Dee bound for Ellesmere on 19th May, 1962. *AMD*

replacement Crosville 'bus, she still had to visit the booking office at Overton-on-Dee to renew her scholar's season ticket! It is unclear if Mr Evans was a station master or a grade one or grade two porter, though in view of the additional wartime freight traffic being handled during this period, it is possible that a man could have been sent out to Overton to assist with the shunting and paper work.

In 1930 Overton-on-Dee issued 6,209 tickets, and in the same year the station dealt with 7,090 tons of goods. By 1932 those figures had dropped to 5,080 tickets and 6,005 tons of freight respectively.

The principal types of freight traffic included domestic coal, sugar beet and agricultural fertilizer, together with animal feed and livestock. The local coal merchants around 1920 were J.H. Billington and W. Davies; coal and other bulk loads were loaded or unloaded in the rear siding or 'coal road', while general merchandise was handled in the 'warehouse road'.

Like other local stations, Overton-on-Dee became much busier during World War II; as we have seen, Overton became the railhead for the American hospitals at Penley, and it also became the site of an army storage and distribution depot that was set up alongside the goods yard in a former factory. A chain link fence was erected around the site and new storage sheds were quickly constructed. This new facility soon became very busy, and it was shunted every other day - usually by the 10.00 am ex-Wrexham goods working.

The traffic was conveyed in covered vans though, as might be expected in wartime conditions, the Great Western train crews 'never knew what came in or what went out!' Jack Wilkinson remembered that there were 'about 20 vans in there at a time', and he normally shunted the yard with '81XX' class large prairie tank No. 8103.

The village of Overton-on-Dee was situated about one mile to the west of the railway in a picturesque riverside setting; the church yard was once famous for its ancient yew trees, which were said locally to have been one of the 'seven wonders of Wales'. There were no railway cartage or lorry services in the Overton area, but there was an arrangement whereby parcels or small freight traffic could be collected or delivered by local carriers.

Cloy Halt

Leaving Overton-on-Dee the single track railway continued northwards, with a minor road running parallel to the right. Trains rumbled beneath a road overbridge before the line reached Cloy Halt. This basic, unstaffed stopping place was opened, apparently as Caedyah Halt, on 30th June, 1932 (although local people cannot remember this name ever appearing on the nameboard); it was closed as a wartime economy measure in June 1940, and re-opened after the war in 1946. The halt consisted of a simple platform on the down side of the line some 5 miles 11 chains from Ellesmere.

The platform was again of earth and timber construction, and it had a length of 75 ft. The waiting shelter provided here was a standard Great Western corrugated iron shed with a low arc roof. A minor road was carried across the line on a single-span brick bridge immediately to the north of the platform.

Overton-on-Dee station viewed from the Ruabon-Whitchurch road with an auto-train in the Ellesmere platform in April 1962. In the distance we can see the chimneys of the brick and tile works (*to the left*) and the CWS milk depot that provided traffic for the railway.   *John M. Strange*

Cloy Halt looking north towards Wrexham on 9th September, 1962.
C.C. Green/John M. Strange Collection

Bangor-on-Dee

Leaving Cloy Halt, trains reached a stretch of embankment that was pierced, at one point, by a minor road bridge. Beyond, the route maintained its northerly heading, and having crossed the A525 motor road on a skew bridge, the railway approached the next stopping place at Bangor-is-y-coed. The station here was known as Bangor-on-Dee; it was 7 miles 36 chains from the starting point of the journey at Ellesmere, although the mile post distance (which was measured from Cambrian Junction) was 7 miles 25 chains.

Bangor-on-Dee station was orientated on a north-south alignment, with cuttings to the south and a road overbridge to the north. Up and down platforms were provided, the main buildings being on the down, or northbound, side. The usual booking office, waiting room and toilet facilities were provided in a small, timber-framed station building that was very similar to its counterpart at neighbouring Overton-on-Dee. The station was attractively situated in a well-wooded, rural setting about a quarter of a mile to the south of the River Dee.

The goods yard, which contained a goods shed, coal wharves, a cattle pen and loading dock, was on the down side. The goods shed was a small, gable-roofed structure of somewhat lightweight construction. There was no yard crane.

The station was fully signalled with up and down home, starting and distant signals. The signal box was another standard Cambrian Railways gabled structure with a brick locking room and a wood and glass operating floor; it was sited at the south end of the up platform, on the opposite side of the line from the station building.

The crossing loop at Bangor-on-Dee was longer than its counterpart at Overton, with a length of 804 ft; there was again, however, an overall speed restriction through the station of 10 mph in each direction.

In staffing terms the situation at Bangor-on-Dee echoed that at Overton - the general picture being one of retraction as the GWR sought ways of reducing staff costs at these rural locations. In the late 1920s the station was supervised by a class five station master, though there were, by that time, just two class five signalmen on the staffing establishment. By the mid-1930s the station master's post had been cut, and Bangor-on-Dee was, thereafter, reduced to a staff of two class five signalmen.

There were no locally-based cartage staff and Bangor-on-Dee was not served by the Ellesmere country lorry service, but in Great Western days parcels and small goods consignments could be collected or delivered by private carriers, who served scattered villages and hamlets such as Worthenbury (two miles from the station), Threapwood (three miles) and Shocklach (four miles), as well as Bangor-on-Dee itself.

In 1923, Bangor-on-Dee booked 11,146 tickets, and there were, in addition, 65 season ticket holders. There was, thereafter, a slight decline in terms of passenger bookings, and by 1930 the station was booking a little over 9,000 tickets per annum; in 1930, for example, annual ticket sales totalled 9,288, while in 1932 there were 9,250 bookings.

Goods traffic showed a somewhat sharper decline, from 9,041 tons in 1923 to 3,796 tons in 1930 and 2,549 by 1932. The traffic handled here was mainly general merchandise, together with a relatively small amount of domestic coal.

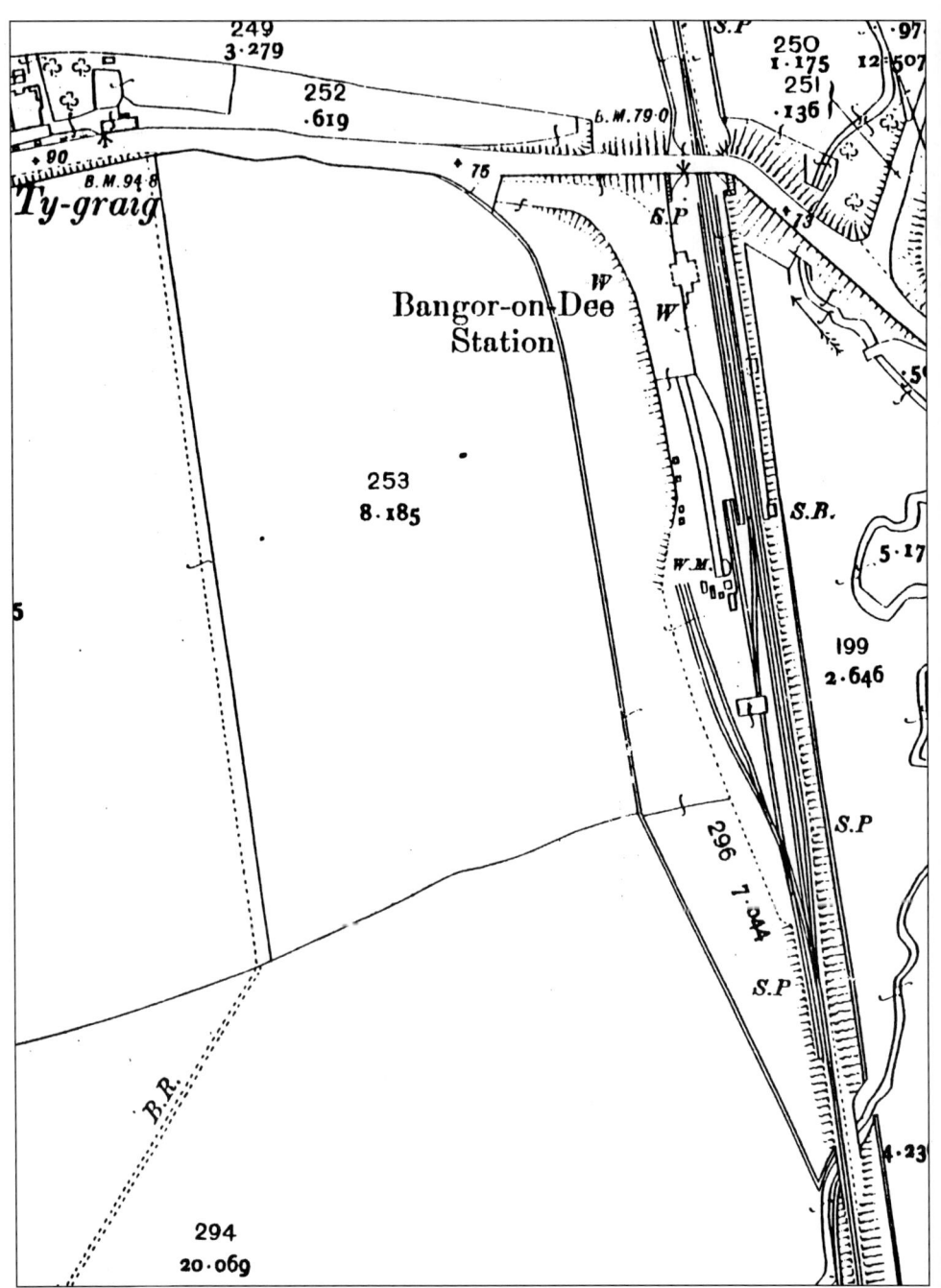

Bangor-on-Dee station. *Reproduced from the 25", 1912 Ordnance Survey Map*

THE STATIONS AND ROUTE FROM ELLESMERE TO SESSWICK

In some years, the station dealt with several large consignments of incoming mineral traffic, which was probably stone or other road-surfacing materials for use on local road-surfacing schemes.

Livestock traffic was a fairly important form of traffic during the 1920s, around 200 wagon loads of cattle being handled at that time. In later years, local farmers turned increasingly to road transport, and this once-significant source of agricultural traffic was then lost forever as far as the railways were concerned.

Although Bangor-on-Dee had no permanent station staff in its later years, there were some locally-based permanent way staff - the Permanent Way gang responsible for the Wrexham & Ellesmere section being stationed here. The ganger in charge of the line during the BR period was F.T. Neal, and his gang included R.V. Martin, who later transferred to Ellesmere where he himself became a ganger on the Whitchurch to Oswestry line.

Sid Barclay, who started his railway career at Bangor-on-Dee in August 1948, initially worked as a lengthman, but after about one year he became a signalman. He worked a two-shift system, the shifts in operation around 1950 being 5.45 am to 1.45 pm, and from 1.45 pm to 9.45 pm. The other signalman was Bill Williams, who had worked at Bangor-on-Dee during the war years with Frank Packham.

Mr Barclay returned to the Engineering Department in the 1950s, and over the years he remembered working with Ken Drury, Erne Suckley and Tommy Davies. As mentioned in *Chapter Three*, the PW gang were equipped with a small inspection trolley and a larger vehicle that could accommodate up to eight men and pull a small trailer carrying tools and other equipment. All three vehicles were stationed at Bangor-on-Dee.

The Appendix to the 1943 Working Timetable shows that the Bangor-on-Dee PW gang were at that time responsible for the entire branch as far south as Cambrian Junction, but Sid Barclay recalled that, in the British Railways period, his gang worked as far south as the station master's house at Overton-on-Dee - beyond which the Ellesmere gang maintained the line.

In addition to maintaining the permanent way, the Bangor-on-Dee gang was responsible for hedge cutting and maintenance along both sides of their section; as Sid Barclay remarks, this amounted to no less than 28 route miles of hedgerows (including the bridge approaches).

Bangor-on-Dee station was conveniently sited within easy walking distance of the River Dee, and for this reason it always attracted a certain amount of 'fishing traffic'. Indeed, as early as November 1895 the *Wrexham Advertiser* reported that it was noticeable that a number of passengers had turned up on Opening Day 'armed with a rod and line'. This, considered the paper, augered very well for the future, and the reporter opined that 'large numbers of anglers' would, in the future, avail themselves of the railway to reach their favourite stretch of river.

Another form of leisure traffic was in connection with race meetings held in the vicinity. Special race trains had been run as far as Wrexham on the Wrexham, Mold & Connah's Quay line prior to the opening of the W&E line in November 1895, and once the Wrexham & Ellesmere line was open these were naturally extended to Bangor-on-Dee. The line had not been ready in time for the April 1895 meeting, but on 10th April, 1896 no less than 3,000 people are said to have travelled through to Bangor station for the races.

Collett '14XX' class 0-4-2T No. 1458 and auto-car at Bangor-on-Dee in 1962 with a train for Ellesmere. Note that, as usual, the locomotive is at the south end of the train. *E.T. Gill*

No. 1458 again at Bangor-on-Dee with an Ellesmere train on 26th May, 1962.

THE STATIONS AND ROUTE FROM ELLESMERE TO SESSWICK

A Wrexham-bound auto-train is signalled to depart from Bangor-on-Dee, with a 14XX' class 0-4-2T providing propulsion on 18th August, 1958. *H. B. Priestley*

The stations on the Wrexham & Ellesmere line had ample platform accommodation, and all three had horse and carriage docks. On race days, large numbers of horse boxes were conveyed to Bangor-on-Dee by passenger train or in special workings, and on such occasions it was necessary for extra staff to be sent out from Oswestry to assist with the shunting.

The village of Bangor-is-y-Coed was three-quarters of a mile to the west of the railway. Bangor was said to have been the site of a great Celtic monastic centre, which is supposed to have been destroyed by the pagan King Aethelfrith of Northumbria in about 607 AD; one of the Bangor-is-y-Coed monks founded another monastery at Bangor on the Menai Straits.

Pickhill Halt and Cadbury's Siding

From Bangor-on-Dee the railway commenced a gentle, north-westwards turn which carried it across a minor road bridge and thence onto the Dee viaduct (7 miles 69 chains). This was the largest engineering feature on the Wrexham & Ellesmere branch, its total length being 66 yards. The bridge was of lattice girder construction, with two bow-shaped girders resting on masonry abutments. It sported a cast-iron plate bearing the legend 'Made & Erected by The Peason & Knowles Coal & Iron Co. Ltd Warrington for the W&ER Co. George Owen Engineer'.

The Dee bridge, looking north-east from the left bank of the river on 9th September, 1962.
C.C. Green/John M. Strange Collection

An auto-train just south of the Dee bridge on 19th May, 1962.

THE STATIONS AND ROUTE FROM ELLESMERE TO SESSWICK

Having crossed the River Dee the line traversed a stretch of raised embankment that kept it well above the surrounding water meadows, and with the exhaust beats of the labouring engine now becoming more distinct, the route began to climb away from the Dee Valley.

Pickhill Halt, the next stop, was 8 miles 56 chains from Ellesmere. It was opened by the GWR on 30th May, 1938 to serve the adjacent Cadbury's Creamery. The passenger platform was situated on the down side, and there was, in addition, a private siding connection to the creamery. The platform was of wooden construction, with a length of 100 ft. For administrative purposes the halt was under the control of Overton-on-Dee station.

Messrs Cadbury Brothers' private siding was on the south side of the line at 8 miles 55 chains. The siding connection was facing to up trains, and the ground frame was locked by the electric train tablet. The line was, at this point, on a rising gradient of 1 in 86, while the first portion of the siding itself fell towards the running line at 1 in 63 (though the remainder of the siding was on the level).

The siding was served by down trains, and by special pilot trips from Bangor-on-Dee. The traffic consisted of up to five van loads of chocolate at a time, together with wagon loads of slack for the boiler house.

Great Western working notices reveal that traffic for the siding was marshalled next to the locomotive, and on arrival at the stop board - which was located 308 yds south of the siding connection - the train was brought to a stand. As it was important that the train would not run back towards Bangor-on-Dee

Pickhill Halt on 9th September, 1962. Note the point just beyond the bridge for Cadbury's private siding looking south towards Ellesmere.   *C.C. Green/John M. Strange Collection*

The private siding which served Cadbury's creamery on 9th September, 1962.
C.C. Green/John M. Strange Collection

when the engine was detached, the guard applied his hand brake before leaving his van; if necessary, he then applied a sufficient number of individual wagon brakes together with (if necessary) one or more sprags to the wheels of the vehicles next to the brake van. When everything was secured, the front portion of the train was uncoupled so that the incoming wagons could be shunted into the siding.

Vehicles from the Cadbury's siding were dropped back onto the stationary part of the train with the engine attached - loose shunting being strictly forbidden on the 1 in 86 gradient; at the same time, train crews were warned that setting back movements should be 'conducted cautiously throughout', with a sufficient number of wagon brakes applied before the setting back movements were commenced.

Sesswick Halt

Sesswick Halt was only a short distance further on at 9 miles 9 chains, and like neighbouring Pickhill Halt, this simple, unstaffed stopping place was on the down side of the running line. The halt was opened by the Cambrian Railways in October 1913, and its facilities consisted of a single 240 ft platform and simple waiting shelter. The shelter was an austere, open-fronted structure, and at night the platform was lit by oil lamps; access from the road overbridge was by means of a sloping path. For administrative purposes the halt was controlled from nearby Marchwiel.

When first opened Sesswick Halt had been equipped with a simple wooden platform, and elderly travellers seem to remember a hand-worked signal which was supposed to be pulled by people wishing for a train to stop! This archaic feature disappeared at an early date, and in Great Western days the halt was substantially rebuilt, with a brick-fronted platform edged with stone slabs. It is believed that the rebuilding was carried out in 1940, when large numbers of construction workers were travelling to and from the halt each day in connection with the nearby Royal Ordnance Factory.

The halt was situated in a cutting, immediately to the south of the B5130 road overbridge. The latter structure was of brick construction and, like the other road overbridges *en route* to Wrexham, it was built with sufficient width to span a double line of rails.

Mr Ron While, who was a young boy during the early years of World War II, confirmed that Sesswick Halt was rebuilt by the GWR in the 1940s, and in a letter to the *Wrexham Leader* he recalled 'literally hundreds' of workers sunning themselves on the grassy banks of the cutting as they waited for the train to take them back to Wrexham in the evening. Many of these would drink beer from bottles which were then discarded along the track - and Mr While would then make 'a small fortune' by collecting these empties and returning them to the Kiln Inn in Cross Lanes for the deposit!

Sesswick Halt looking north towards Wrexham during the 1960s. After rebuilding in World War II, Sesswick was provided with a 240 ft platform. *S.C. Jenkins/Lens of Sutton Collection*

A view from the footplate of Collett '14XX' class 0-4-2T No. 1432, arriving at Sesswick Halt with the 1.30 pm from Wrexham Central on 1st May, 1962. *John White*

Chapter Five

The Stations and Route From Sesswick to Wrexham

From Sesswick Halt the Wrexham & Ellesmere line continued its climb through further cuttings, on a 1 in 101 rising gradient. Passing beneath a further road overbridge, northbound trains reached the crossing loop at Marchwiel Factory.

Marchwiel Royal Ordnance Factory Sidings

As we have seen, this large, rail-connected ordnance depot was established on a site to the north of the railway in 1940, access from the running line being controlled by a 72-lever signal box on the up side at 9 miles 34 chains. The private siding connection was probably ready for use by August 1940, the first traffic being in the form of construction materials, as the Royal Ordnance Factory itself was not in production until the following November.

The sidings were entered via a connection that was facing to up trains, a loop being provided where the private line diverged from the main line.

The loop at Marchwiel Factory was 1,200 ft long, and it could be used for crossing purposes as well as running-round. There were various facilities within the factory area, including a passenger platform for military use, and a five-road marshalling yard; the latter was equipped with a water column and a short brake van siding. In 1943 the marshalling sidings were numbered in sequence from one to five - Nos. 1 to 4 being used for incoming traffic while siding No. 5 was normally used for out-going traffic from the ordnance factory. Incoming trains were propelled into the marshalling yard by Great Western engines, while factory shunters placed out-going vehicles on siding No. 5.

At a later stage of the war, the number of marshalling sidings was increased to about 10 roads, each of which was about a quarter of a mile in length. One of these sidings was used by the Central Wagon Repair Company as a cripple road, and wagons were sometimes brought into the works for repair.

Other types of incoming traffic included coal, sulphur and other chemicals, while outwards traffic included repaired wagons, empties, vans of cordite, and mysterious sealed vans that no doubt contained other lethal products of the ordnance factory. The cordite was usually taken on from Ellesmere to Crewe by the 1.15 Oswestry to Crewe Gresty Lane goods working - this early morning service being typically worked by a Collett '2251' class 0-6-0 tender locomotive.

The Marchwiel Factory employed both steam and diesel locomotives on its extensive internal system - the diesels being particularly useful when dealing with explosives.

The steam engines were of various makes and vintages. One of the oldest locomotives used on the site was an 0-4-0ST known as *Victory*, which dated from as far back as 1859; this veteran saddle tank was later transferred to the Shropshire & Montgomeryshire Railway. Other steam engines used during the construction of the ROF included the saddle tanks *Mombasa* and *Thika*, but it is

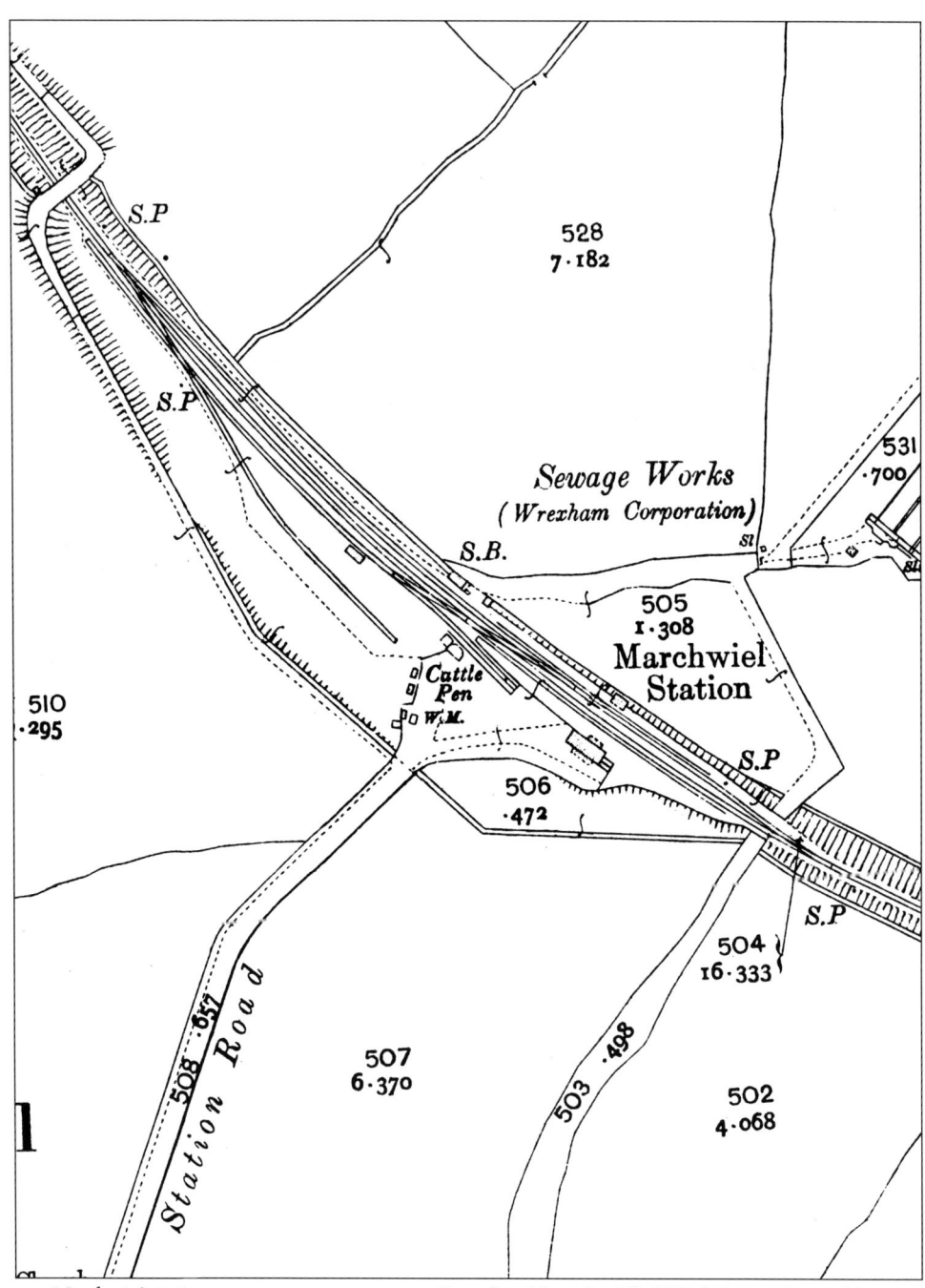

Marchwiel station. *Reproduced from the 25", 1909 Ordnance Survey Map*

THE STATIONS AND ROUTE FROM SESSWICK TO WREXHAM 97

believed that these contractor's locomotives were transferred to other sites when building work at Marchwiel was complete.

In general, the ROF system was worked by diesels, a fleet of two Hawthorn, two Hunslet and one Barclay internal combustion engines being employed on the Marchwiel Factory site. There was, in addition, an internal 2 ft 6 in. gauge network with its own battery-electric locomotives.

Marchwiel

Now heading north-westwards, the single line approached Marchwiel (10 miles 35 chains) which, like Overton and Bangor-on-Dee, was a passing place with up and down platforms and full goods facilities for coal, livestock and general merchandise traffic. A private goods siding known as Five Fords Siding was situated a short distance to the south of the station at 10 miles 5 chains.

The track layout at Marchwiel incorporated a 771 ft crossing loop, with the main station buildings and goods yard on the down side. The goods sidings were entered via a trailing connection from the down main line, and there was also a connection from the up main line that left the running line in a trailing connection and crossed the down line on the level in order to reach the yard; a single slip arrangement gave access from the up main to the down main line, and this connection was useful when down goods trains called *en route*, and had to run-round their trains in order to pick-up or set-down in the goods yard.

The goods yard itself contained a fan of dead-end sidings, one of which terminated in an end-loading dock behind the down platform, while another served a cattle loading dock; there was no yard crane.

Marchwiel's diminutive wooden station building was clearly in the same architectural family as its neighbours at Overton and Bangor-on-Dee. The basic timber-framed structure was clad in horizontal lapped weather boarding, and the low-pitch gabled roof was covered in Welsh slates. The platform facade featured a centrally-placed doorway flanked by pairs of windows on each side. A single chimney stack with two flues extended above the roof, and there was a small projecting canopy.The latter was supported by ornamented wooden brackets, and the edge of the canopy was adorned by 'egg-and-hole' shaped valancing. The interior layout at Marchwiel station provided the usual accommodation for staff and travellers. The ticket office was situated at the right-hand end of the building (when viewed from the platform), while the general waiting room occupied the central part of the structure. The ladies' waiting room was sited to the left of the waiting room, while the gentlemen's urinal was housed in a small extension at the south end.

Other buildings at Marchwiel included a small waiting shelter on the up platform, and a typical Cambrian Railways-style gabled signal cabin, the latter being situated at the north end of the up platform. In common with many other Cambrian boxes it was of brick and timber construction with a distinctive 'cut away' porch at one end; it boasted scalloped barge boards, decorative finials and a startlingly-tall chimney stack that rose from the rear wall of the structure (this eventually became unsafe, and it was then replaced by a very long stove pipe chimney).

Marchwiel station from the station approach in April 1962. *John M. Strange*

Marchwiel station looking towards Wrexham a few months after closure to passengers. The Cambrian-style gable-roofed signal cabin can be glimpsed to the right of the picture.

S.C. Jenkins/Lens of Sutton Collection

Collett '74XX' 0-6-0PT No. 7405 stands in the up platform at Marchwiel with a Wrexham to Ellesmere working. An unidentified '57XX' class 0-6-0PT waits in the down platform line with a local freight service. The '74XX' class 0-6-0PTs were not auto-fitted, and when they were employed on the branch passenger service it was necessary for running-round to take place at the end of each journey. *S.C. Jenkins/Lens of Sutton Collection*

Quite a busy scene as Collett 0-4-2T No. 1458 stands at Marchwiel with a train for Ellesmere on 26th May, 1962.

Marchwiel goods yard, looking north, on 9th September, 1962, showing the cattle pens and signal box. *C.C. Green/John M. Strange Collection*

Marchwiel station looking towards Wrexham shortly after the withdrawal of passenger services. The goods yard is occupied by 16 ton mineral wagons. *S.C. Jenkins/Lens of Sutton Collection*

At night, the station was lit by oil lamps resting in tapering glass lanterns, some of which were supported by lamp posts while others were simply bolted to convenient buildings or telegraph poles. The platforms were fenced with a mix of pale-and-space and post-and-rail fencing.

At the time of the Grouping Marchwiel station had a staff of four, though in the late 1920s the staffing establishment had been reduced to one grade one porter and two class five signalmen. By 1934, there were just two class five signalmen at this relatively obscure outpost - though additional staff were needed in World War II when the new signal box was opened at nearby Marchwiel Factory.

The station typically booked about 5,000 tickets a year during the 1930s, some 4,790 tickets being issued in 1930, while 5,189 were sold in 1932. Goods traffic amounted to no more than 1,132 tons in 1930, rising very slightly to 1,636 tons by 1932. Later, however, the establishment of Marchwiel ordnance factory resulted in a tremendous upsurge in goods traffic through Marchwiel Factory Siding - though Marchwiel station handled no more than occasional consignments of coal and bricks.

Five Fords Farm Siding

Five Fords Siding, which was sited on the up side of the running line about a quarter of a mile to the south of the passenger station, was one of the first private sidings to have been installed on the Wrexham & Ellesmere line, a private siding agreement having been signed on 20th January, 1904. The siding was initially used mainly for agricultural products - 'garden produce' being the official description of the traffic handled here. This siding was, at one time, used by a firm trading as Bellis Brothers, though the Ministry of Supply assumed control during World War II.

The siding was entered via a connection facing towards Ellesmere, and for this reason it was usually shunted by up trains; if necessary, an engine could be sent out light from Marchwiel station to collect traffic from the siding, in which case the wagons concerned would be propelled along the line towards Marchwiel. The siding was worked from a ground frame locked by the electric train tablet.

Five Fords Siding remained in use during the British Railways period, but the private siding agreement was finally terminated on 31st December, 1955. It is doubtful if the siding saw much traffic in its final years, though, when used by Bellis Brothers, potatoes, cabbages and seasonal fruit produce was dispatched regularly to Liverpool, Manchester and other large cities in sacks or hampers. The siding itself was a short, dead-end spur holding no more than about half a dozen wagons; a gate was kept closed across the line until such time as the siding was shunted.

After Marchwiel, down trains climbed steadily north-westwards through a landscape that showed more traces of industry as the line neared Wrexham. At Forge Mill (11 miles 12 chains) the railway crossed the 34 yard Forge Mill viaduct.

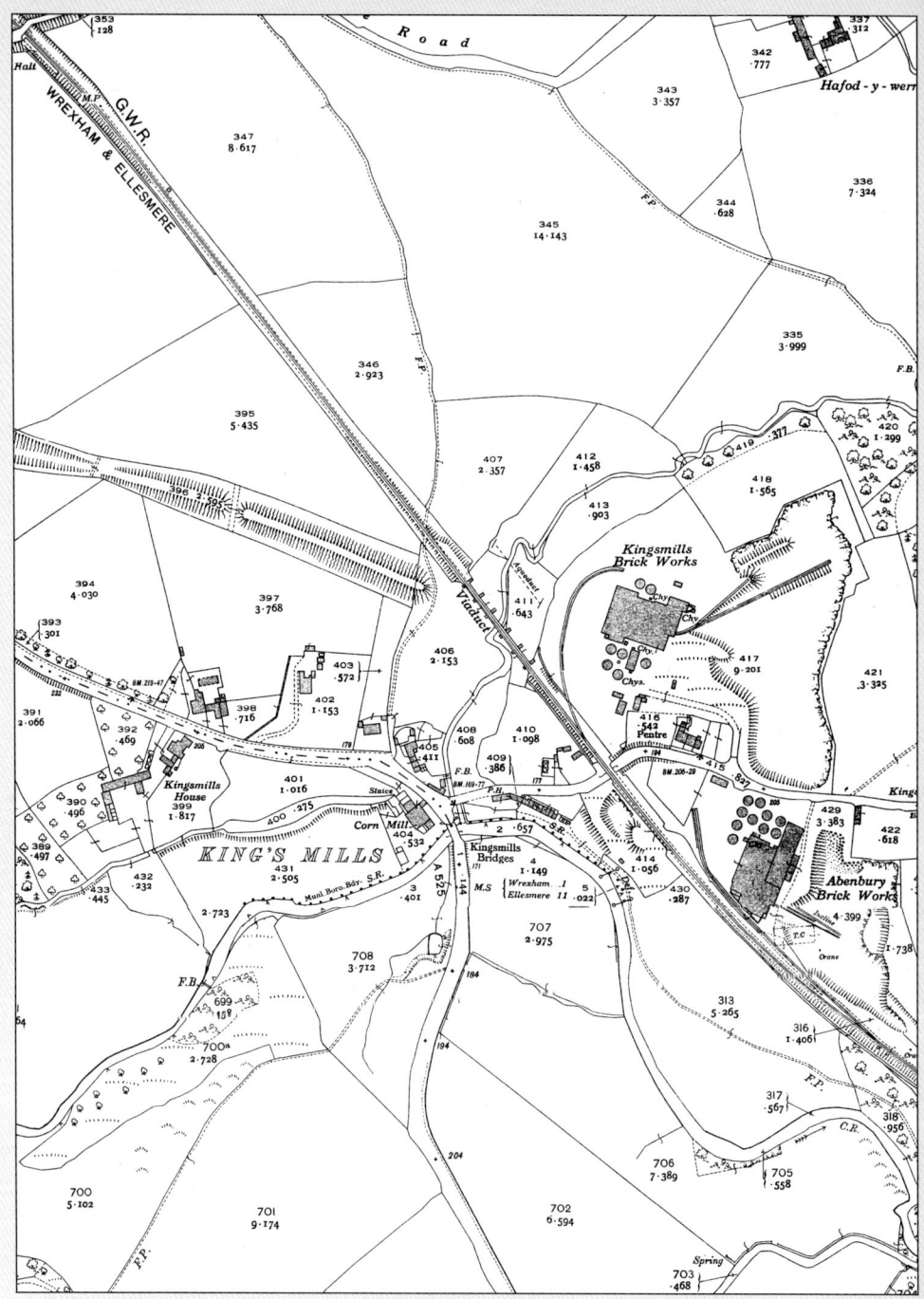

Kings Mill and Abenbury brickworks, notice also Kings Mill viaduct and the unfinished earthworks of the Wrexham, Mold & Connah's Quay Railway extension to Whitchurch to the west of the Wrexham & Ellesmere line. Hightown Halt is at the top of the map with access from the road overbridge adjacent.
Reproduced from the 25", 1937 Ordnance Survey Map

THE STATIONS AND ROUTE FROM SESSWICK TO WREXHAM

Abenbury Brick Works Siding

There were further private sidings on this northernmost section of the Wrexham & Ellesmere line, including Abenbury Siding (11 miles 25 chains) and Kings Mill Siding (11 miles 40 chains). Both of these sidings were entered by means of connections that were facing to down trains; they were worked from ground frames locked by the electric train tablet for the Marchwiel to Wrexham Central single line section.

Abenbury brick works siding had originated as a construction depot used by Messrs Davies Brothers during the building of the Wrexham & Ellesmere line. Davies Brothers leased the land upon which the brick works was built from Thomas Lloyd Fitzhugh of Plas Power, in 1892. In 1899, the works employed 125 men, each of whom earned £ 1 per week.

The siding was later worked under a private siding agreement made with the Oughtibridge Silica Firebrick Company of Sheffield. The 1937 25 inch Ordnance Survey map shows 10 brick kilns beside a single, dead-end siding (as opposed to three sidings on the 1898 Ordnance Survey map). A large clay pit is shown to the east of the brick plant.

In the 1940s, Abenbury Siding was used to convey wagons of china clay to the brick works, together with loads of locally-produced slack coal for the furnaces. Outwards traffic consisted only of empty wagons, as all of the completed bricks were sent out in road vehicles.

Abenbury and Kings Mill sidings were, in general, worked by up freight trains, which could leave their brake vans and rear portions on the running line and then draw forward before shunting back into the sidings; a notice board was set up beside Abenbury siding to indicate the point beyond which engines were not to proceed. As both sidings were sited on gradients that fell towards Marchwiel, it was necessary for trains to be secured by the guard's brake and a sufficient number of wagon brakes before engines were uncoupled to shunt the sidings.

If necessary, traffic for Abenbury or Kings Mill sidings could be propelled from Marchwiel station - a brake van or 'other suitable vehicle' being marshalled at the rear of the train. Photographic evidence shows that, in BR days, brake vans were often dispensed with during these operations, though it was still necessary for the guard or shunter to travel in the leading vehicle during propelling movements so that a good lookout could be kept.

Kings Mill Brick Works Siding

Kings Mill (or Kingsmills) brick works was literally next door to Abenbury brick works, being separated from it by the Kingsmills Road. Kings Mill brick works had been founded in 1885 by Edward Meredith Jones, a local builder and timber merchant. The 1898 Ordnance Survey map shows that the works had four brick kilns, together with an inclined tramway which extended from the brick plant to an adjacent clay pit.

Internal Great Western documents reveal that a private siding agreement was made between the Cambrian Railways and the Wrexham Brick & Tile Company

Above: Kings Mill viaduct in 1960, looking north, with part of the Rubery Owen factory in the distance.
  C.C. Green/John M. Strange Collection

Right: Detail of Kings Mill viaduct on 8th September, 1962; note that the piers were wide enough to accommodate a double track formation.
  C.C. Green/John M. Strange Collection

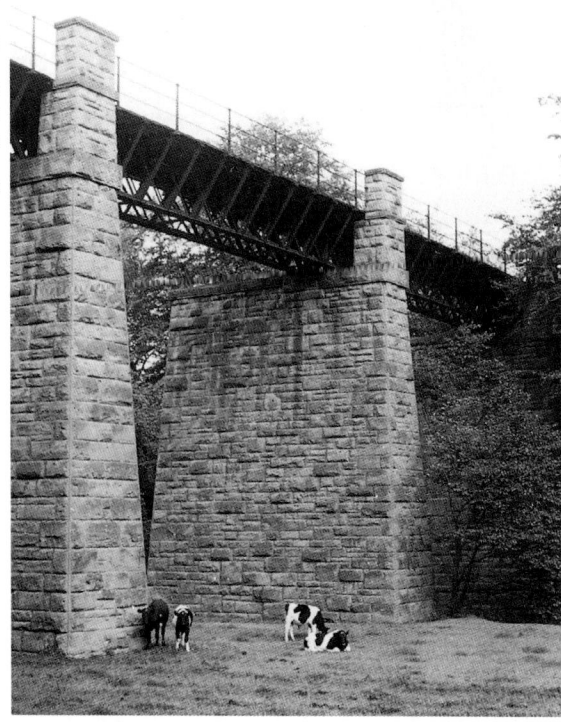

on 24th July, 1914, and it is assumed that the Kings Mill Siding was opened shortly afterwards. This facility is shown on the 1937 Ordnance Survey map as a single, dead-end siding that curved away from the east side of the running line. Its total length was about 7½ chains; nearby, the brick works had grown into a seven kiln plant, while the clay pit had, by that time, been greatly expanded.

The Great Western Railway *Register of Private Sidings* lists the principal form of traffic at Kings Mill Siding as 'bricks', and this is confirmed by Jack Wilkinson, who affirmed that wagon loads of bricks were shunted out 'about twice a week' by up trains *en route* from Wrexham; inwards traffic consisted of 'empty wagons' - presumably because the brick works obtained all its clay on site.

Climbing past Kings Mill Siding on a 1 in 304 rising gradient, trains soon crossed the 84 yard Kings Mill viaduct at 11 miles 45 chains. This five-span structure consisted of lattice girders supported by substantial masonry piers; the piers were wide enough to accommodate two lines, although the sinuous girders were for single track only.

The Kings Mill area was also of interest in that it marked the site of the unfinished earthworks of the abortive Wrexham, Mold & Connah's Quay extension to Whitchurch, which would be glimpsed to the left as trains crossed the viaduct. Although abandoned as long ago as the 1870s, the WM&CQ line was clearly defined; the massive embankment would have given access to a viaduct across the Clywedog and Gwenfro rivers that would have stood roughly on the same site as the later Wrexham & Ellesmere viaduct. The completed section of embankment was about 410 yards long, and if the line had been completed it would have continued westwards from the Wrexham & Ellesmere route in order to pass to the south of Wrexham, whereas the W&E line took a more northerly route to enter the town centre.

Hightown Siding and Halt

Still heading north-westwards, the line ran more or less parallel to the A525 road as it neared Wrexham. Soon, the factory chimneys of Wrexham itself could be seen in the distance, together with the distinctive tower of St Giles' church, which dominated the entire scene. A small halt was provided at Hightown to serve the industrial eastern suburbs of the town. This halt, which was situated on the down side at 11 miles 74 chains, was opened shortly after the Grouping on 9th July, 1923.

The halt consisted of an earth and timber platform, with a lamp, nameboard, notice board and a simple waiting shelter; the platform was 98 ft long. Rubery Owens engineering works, which was originally built in 1941 as an aircraft components factory, was on the up side. Although Hightown was an unstaffed stopping place with no sidings or other connections, there was a private siding to the wartime factory just under a quarter of a mile to the south at 11 miles 55 chains. This facility was connected to the running line by a siding connection that was facing to the direction of down trains.

'14XX' class 0-4-2T No. 1458 coasts into Hightown Halt with the 1.25 pm Wrexham-Ellesmere service on 6th June, 1960. *J.M. Oldham*

'14XX' class 0-4-2T No 1438 pulls away from Hightown Halt on 18th April, 1960, with the 4.20 pm train from Ellesmere. The trackbed here is now a footpath. *M. Mensing*

Wrexham (Caia) Goods Yard

Having entered the outskirts of Wrexham, the line ran through a built-up area, with the Willow Brewery visible to the left, together with a large leather factory and the town's gas works. These local industries were not served directly by rail sidings, but their transport needs were catered for by the provision of a goods depot known as Caia Road goods station (12 miles 28 chains). This consisted of a number of coal and general merchandise sidings on the up side, and its facilities included cattle pens and a 1 ton 10 cwt yard crane.

Caia goods yard was linked to the running line by two ground frames, one of which was at the east end of the yard while the other was at the west. The siding connections were unlocked by the electric train tablet.

The yard was served by up and down services, the usual practice being for up trains to work traffic into the east (Marchwiel) end of the yard while down trains worked the west (Wrexham) end; special short distance workings were also worked from Wrexham Central, propelling movements being permitted provided that there was a brake van or other suitable vehicle with a guard keeping a sharp lookout.

Additionally, Caia goods yard was linked to Wrexham Central passenger station by a long headshunt on the up side, which extended into the station on a parallel alignment. The 1943 Appendix to Section 16 of the Working Timetable reveals that this parallel line was treated as a siding or shunting neck, for which reason a wheel stop was locked across the line at the Caia end. If, for any reason, it was necessary for shunting movements to take place between Caia goods yard and Wrexham Central station (or vice versa) the wheel stop could be unlocked by a key that was normally kept in Wrexham Central signal box - thereby allowing unobstructed movements to take place over the headshunt line.

Caia goods yard took its name from Caia Road - which, in turn was named after Caia Farm. The 1898 Ordnance Survey map shows just two dead-end sidings entered from the Wrexham direction, though by the 1930s three sidings were in existence, one of these being a loop with connections at each end (in effect an extension of the headshunt from Wrexham Central). The other two sidings were dead-end roads, one of which terminated alongside the cattle dock.

The principal sources of traffic handled at Caia Road goods yard were scrap iron for Brymbo and Shotton steel works, and domestic coal for local coal merchants. A small goods shed was situated on the loop siding, near the entrance to the yard from Caia Road. The goods depot occupied an elevated site, the premises of the Cambrian Leather Works, on the south side of the line, being at a lower level; Salop Road passed under the railway via an underline bridge at the west end of the goods yard.

Wrexham Central

Nearing their destination, down trains rumbled over the 69 yard Willow Road viaduct, and with St Giles' church now clearly visible on the right-hand side of the line, the 12½ mile journey from Ellesmere was almost at an end. Slowing to a crawl, trains rumbled over Town Hill on another lengthy bridge, and then came to a stand in the through platforms at Wrexham Central station (12 miles 57 chains).

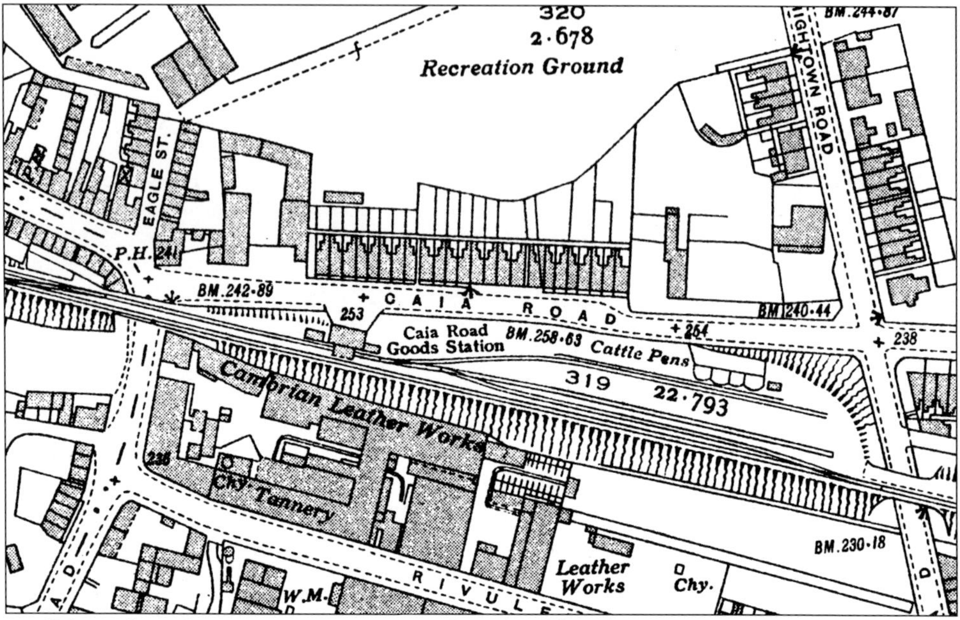

Caia goods yard.

Reproduced from the 25", 1937 Ordnance Survey Map

Caia goods yard, looking towards Ellesmere on 8th September, 1962; wagons are being loaded with scrap metal in the background. *C.C. Green/John M. Strange Collection*

THE STATIONS AND ROUTE FROM SESSWICK TO WREXHAM 109

Wrexham Central, the northern terminus of the Wrexham & Ellesmere branch, was also the southernmost extremity of the Wrexham, Mold & Connah's Quay Railway, the facilities being shared between the Cambrian and Great Central companies. The station was orientated on a roughly east to west alignment, Cambrian services being handled on the south or down side, while Great Central trains terminated on the up side.

Five platform faces were provided, the main up and down lines used by trains to and from Ellesmere being in the centre, while two terminal bays on the north side were used by Wrexham, Mold & Connah's Quay services; an additional bay was available on the down side.

There was a relatively large goods yard to the west of the passenger station, with all of the usual facilities including coal wharves, cattle pens and a large brick-built goods shed. Until 1922 the Cambrian Railways had made use of a small engine shed on the down side of the line, but in 1926 this prefabricated structure was moved to a new site at Aberayron.

The platforms at Wrexham Central were wide and spacious, but this served only to accentuate the comparatively sparse passenger facilities; small and somewhat mean single-storey buildings were provided on both sides, the building on the down side being of timber construction while its counterpart on the up side was built of corrugated iron. Both of these structures sported small canopies, but the platforms were otherwise uncovered. The up and down sides of the station were linked by a lattice girder footbridge. There was, in addition, a small wooden station building on the centre platform, with canopies on both of its facades.

When first opened to public traffic in 1887 Wrexham Central had been a simple, single track terminus. The Wrexham, Mold & Connah's Quay line was doubled in the following year, but the station remained an essentially small-scale establishment until the opening of the Wrexham & Ellesmere route in 1895. Subsequent development was limited by the restricted site upon which the station had been constructed - a major impediment to further growth being the massive bulk of St Mark's church, which loomed over the goods yard in the vicinity of the goods shed. The church had been consecrated, as an Anglican chapel-of-ease, on 21st May, 1858.

In its fully developed form, the station consisted of the double-tracked Wrexham, Mold & Connah's Quay main line, which swept through the centre of the complex in a great 'S' bend; the Wrexham & Ellesmere line converged with this main line immediately to the west of the platforms, the junction provided being (in later years at least) a conventional double track intersection. The platforms were numbered in sequence from one to five, platform one, on the north side of the station, being known as 'No. 1 Bay', while the other terminal road on the Wrexham, Mold & Connah's Quay side of the station was known as 'No. 2 Bay'. The two through platforms were known as platforms three and four, while the down side bay was designated platform five.

There was a parallel goods line on the north side, and this terminated in a fan of dead-end sidings beside the WM&CQ platforms; the goods shed was served by a loop siding that ran parallel to the main goods line, and there were further dead-end goods sidings on the east side of Bradley Road bridge. The latter structure was a long, brick and plate girder overbridge which carried Bradley Road across the entire site from north to south.

A panoramic view of Wrexham Central station, taken from the roof of St Giles' church tower in 1952. An Ellesmere auto-train is in the platform nearest the camera. Further along the platform is a six-coach set which would form a working to Seacombe and be worked by former LNER engines off Rhosddu shed. In the bay platform stands another four-coach set. In the background can be seen the goods shed, and beyond the road bridge is the Chester to Shrewsbury main line. Town Hill viaduct is visible in the foreground, and St Mark's church can be seen in the background. Meanwhile in Brook Street two Crosville buses and a Bedford OB from a private operator can be seen. *Wrexham Leader*

THE STATIONS AND ROUTE FROM SESSWICK TO WREXHAM

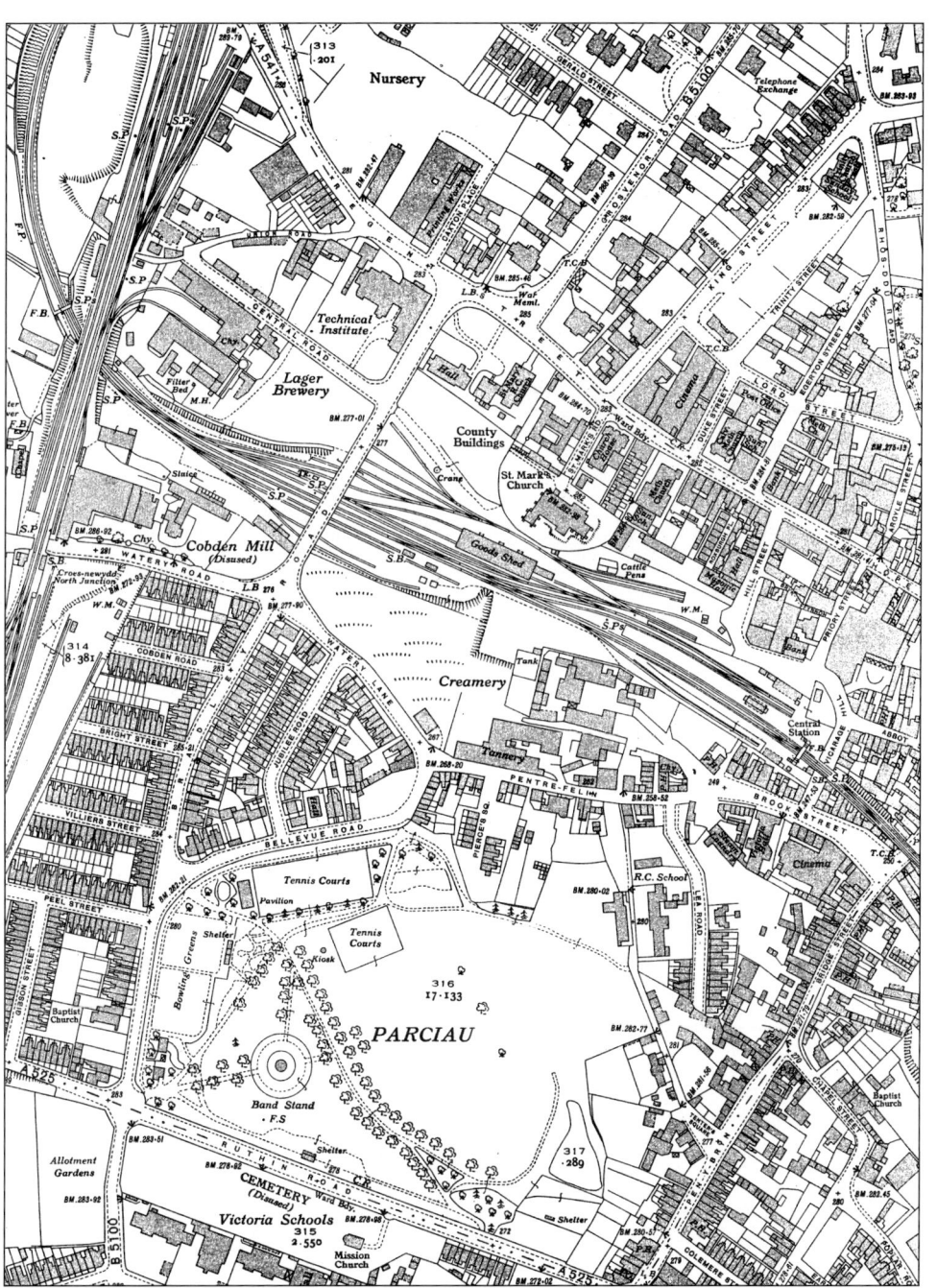

Wrexham Central station and goods yard.   *Reproduced from the 25", 1937 Ordnance Survey Map*

An auto-train for Elllesmere departs from Wrexham Central on 25th August, 1962. St Giles' church dominates the skyline. The chimneys of the Willow brewery can also been seen in the distance.

Wrexham Central looking west from platform 1. The substantial brick goods shed can be seen in the distance, together with Bradley Road overbridge. The old Island Green brewery, which closed in the 1930s, is on the left. The station site is now a shopping centre and a new central station is part of the complex.
S.C. Jenkins/Lens of Collection

THE STATIONS AND ROUTE FROM SESSWICK TO WREXHAM   113

The sidings on the south side of the main WM&CQ running lines included a link to Cobden's extensive flour mills - which were also served by a connection from the adjacent GWR main line which, at this point, passed over the Wrexham, Mold & Connah's Quay route on a substantial girder bridge.

In Cambrian Railways days, there had been a 50 ft diameter engine turntable near the Wrexham & Ellesmere platforms, this facility being reached by means of a siding connection from the up (Cambrian) main line that crossed the down line on the level; the turntable was removed after the Grouping - by which time, of course, push-pull working had obviated the need for engines to be turned at the end of each journey from Ellesmere.

Wrexham Central was signalled from a wooden GCR-type gable-roofed signal box on the down side of the line, and a Cambrian signal box at the east end of the station. Minor details included a small single-storey hut on the up side, together with a lengthy open-fronted bicycle shed. Locomotives were able to replenish their tanks from a single water column at the west end of the terminal platforms on the up side.

Wrexham Central remained, in effect, a 'joint' station until Nationalisation in 1948, and even in BR days, the continued use of Robinson 'C13' class 4-4-2Ts (and other former Great Central types) on the WM&CQ route imparted a lingering pre-Grouping atmosphere. In later years, the signals on the Wrexham, Mold & Connah's Quay side of the station were replaced by standard LMS upper quadrants, but Great Western lower quadrants were retained on the Wrexham & Ellesmere side.

The station was under the control of an LNER station master in the 1930s, though in earlier years the Cambrian Railways and the Wrexham, Mold & Connah's Quay companies had maintained separate staffing establishments. Great Western staff returns reveal that by 1931 the only GWR employees at Wrexham Central were two signalmen who worked in the South box; they were supervised by the LNER station master.

The first station master at Wrexham Central was probably Tom Johnson, who is mentioned in the 1895 *Bennett's Directory* and is likely to have been in charge of the station since its opening just seven years before. One of the last station masters here was Reginald Alfred Webster, whose term of office lasted from 1950 until 1964.

While on the subject of Wrexham Central station, it would be of interest to mention that, when first proposed in the 1880s, the station was referred to as Wrexham 'Jubilee'. On 25th June, 1887 the *Wrexham Advertiser* published a special supplement, and this souvenir edition included a panoramic drawing of the new station, which showed the WM&CQ extension from Wrexham Exchange, the 'Jubilee Station', and the hoped-for continuation towards Ellesmere.

The proposed Jubilee station was similar to the station that was actually being built, albeit slightly further to the east. The station was depicted as a high-level affair, with substantially-built booking offices and waiting rooms on each side. As proposed in June 1887 the station would have been carried on raised arches for much of its length, with a covered stairway to Town Hill and a subway connection from Brook Street. The Old Vicarage was shown as a sort of annex to the main station buildings, suggesting that there may have been some thought of

'14XX' class No. 1458 at Overton-on-Dee in 1962. *E.T. Gill*

A '14XX' propels its auto-coach away from Pickhill Halt on 19th May, 1962. *AMD*

The line was closed as planned with effect from 10th September, 1962, and as this was a Monday, the last scheduled passenger trains ran on Saturday 8th September, 1962. On that day the stations and halts at Elson, Trench, Overton-on-Dee, Cloy, Bangor-on-Dee, Pickhill, Sesswick and Hightown were closed in their entirety.

The Last Trains

The closure of the Wrexham & Ellesmere Railway was commemorated in the usual way, and many people turned up to participate in the closure proceedings. Paradoxically, the doomed line was busier on its last day than it had been for many years, and it is clearly a pity that those who travelled on the branch on this final day of operation could not have done so with greater regularity before the closure was announced!

The final day was treated as a normal operating day, and the regular timetable remained in force. Collett '14XX' class 0-4-2T No. 1432, an engine that had worked the line for three decades, was rostered for duties on the branch passenger service, and the morning and early afternoon passed without much incident. Many extra travellers rode on the line, while little knots of photographers and well-wishers were in evidence as the push-pull train glided up and down the branch.

As darkness fell, the numbers of spectators appeared to diminish, but the crowds started to gather at Wrexham Central in greater numbers as the end approached.

It was expected that many people would wish to travel on the very last scheduled train and, in consequence, the final 9.00 pm service from Wrexham was strengthened to four coaches. The train consisted of two auto-trailers, to which had been added two ordinary coaches - the resulting ensemble being a considerable load for the four-coupled locomotive, which would normally have hauled no more than one (or occasionally) two trailers on the Wrexham & Ellesmere route.

The final train left Wrexham with over 200 last-day travellers on board and, whistling frequently, it set off into the September night. Soon, the street lights of Wrexham had been left far behind, and the brightly-lit train was running through open countryside. Little could be seen as the '14XX' laboured through pitch-black fields with its unusually heavy load, though groups of people had gathered at the stations to pay their last respects. The engine was driven by George Wilkinson from Oswestry, who had worked on the W&E line since 1918, and the passengers included Alderman Herbert Hampson, who, as a boy, had travelled on the first train into Wrexham.

At Marchwiel, the train set off a barrage of detonators that had been placed on the rails, while at Overton-on-Dee there was a considerable delay when the communication cord was pulled. Resuming its sad, final journey, the train toiled out of the Dee Valley - the sharp staccato beat of the engine being heard for many miles across the fields. At last the '14XX' and its packed four-coach train reached Ellesmere, where, almost half an hour later than planned, the final scheduled passenger journey between Wrexham and Ellesmere came to an end.

The token is handed to the footplate crew on '14XX' No. 1432 at Bangor-on-Dee on 19th May, 1962. *AMD*

The fireman looks out from the cab of No. 1458 in this view at Marchwiel in 1962. *E.T. Gill*

THE FINAL YEARS : 1948-1982

A Wrexham train departs from Overton-on-Dee on 19th May, 1962.

Collett '14XX' No. 1458 waits at Ellesmere in 1962 prior to its next trip on the auto-train service to Wrexham. Notice the wooden step provided to ease boarding for the train's passengers.

E.T. Gill

An unidentified '57XX' class 0-6-0PT heads northwards from Overton-on-Dee with a mixed freight working during the 1960s.
John M. Strange

Propelling movements were allowed on the Wrexham & Ellesmere branch in connection with the various private sidings *en route* to Wrexham; here an unidentified '57XX' class 0-6-0PT propels a rake of about 12 wooden-bodied open wagons towards Abenbury and Kings Mill sidings. The destination is probably Kings Mill brickworks, the usual practice being for empties to be shunted into the siding for loading. The guard or shunter keeping a lookout in the leading wagon is believed to be Paddy Boyd.
John M. Strange

THE FINAL YEARS : 1948-1982

A Freight-Only Branch

The remaining infrastructure was modified for freight-only working in the weeks following closure, and by November 1962 the branch had officially been cut back to Cadbury's Siding (Pickhill), which then became the southernmost limit of operation.

In practice, the line continued a little way beyond Pickhill Halt, the official 'end' of the goods-only line being at a point 8 miles 48½ chains from Ellesmere - at which place a stop block was set up. As Pickhill siding diverged from the running line at 8 miles 55 chains, this meant that about 430 ft of track remained *in situ* as a siding for use when traffic was worked in or out of the creamery.

The surviving portion of the Wrexham & Ellesmere route was (1962) worked by electric train token by between Wrexham and Marchwiel, but the truncated spur to Cadbury's Creamery was reduced to one-engine-in-steam working. Caia goods yard remained in use, together with Marchwiel Factory, Abenbury, Kings Mill and Hightown private sidings. Facilities for full wagon load traffic were retained at Marchwiel.

The now-closed line between Ellesmere and Pickhill was subsequently lifted, but the industrialised northern part of the branch remained relatively busy. Indeed, this surviving section saw at least some bulk freight workings, a notable visitor in this context being BR Standard '9F' class 2-10-0 No. 92122, which hauled an experimental block oil working to Marchwiel Factory on 26th July, 1966. The locomotive returned light to Wrexham at the end of the trip, having made history in that it was the largest locomotive to have visited the Wrexham & Ellesmere branch at that time.

Meanwhile, as the pace of closure and retraction gathered momentum, the connecting lines at each end of the erstwhile Wrexham & Ellesmere Railway were themselves marked down for closure under the notorious 'Beeching Plan'.

Published in March 1963, the Beeching proposals - euphemistically entitled *The Reshaping of British Railways* - envisaged the withdrawal of passenger services from 5,000 route miles of railway, together with the closure of 2,363 stations. Duplicate routes would be eliminated, while wagon load and sundries freight traffic would be severely reduced; on a more positive note, the Beeching Plan also advocated the development of bulk freight traffic and the improvement of inter-city passenger routes.

As far as the local railway system was concerned these proposals presaged doom for both the Whitchurch-Oswestry-Welshpool routes *and* the former WM&CQ route from Wrexham to Birkenhead. Perversely, however, the news was not quite so bad for the remaining portion of the Wrexham & Ellesmere line which, as a freight-only route serving private sidings, seemed to have found a niche in the post-Beeching railway system.

The withdrawal of passenger services between Wrexham Central, Chester and New Brighton was first threatened in November 1965, but this proposal faced a storm of protest, and the closure was not immediately implemented. In the interim, the election of a Labour Government had resulted in a perceptibly less hostile environment for the nationalised railways.

The wooden station building at Overton-on-Dee looking south along the down platform. Although taken during demolition of the line during the mid-1960s, this view reveals some useful details of the building. A small Andrew Barclay diesel shunter employed on demolition work stands in the platform road. *S.C. Jenkins/Lens of Sutton Collection*

A desolate scene at Cloy Halt looking north towards Wrexham after the removal of track.
S.C. Jenkins/Lens of Sutton Collection

THE FINAL YEARS : 1948-1982   133

Labour politicians were less inclined to implement large scale railway closures for purely economic reasons, and there was now more interest in the concept of state subsidies for socially-necessary routes. Thus, in March 1968, Transport Minister Barbara Castle decided that closure of the Wrexham to New Brighton line would be deferred (although the closure of the Chester to Dee Marsh Junction route was allowed to proceed).

Conductor-guard operation was introduced on the Wrexham, Mold & Connah's Quay line on Sunday 20th April, 1969, and in June the Minister of Transport agreed that the line would continue in operation supported by a social grant. The Minister did, on the other hand, indicate that both Wrexham Central and Wrexham Exchange stations might be closed, so that all of the town's railway services could be diverted into the nearby former Great Western station (Wrexham General).

Further proposals for the closure of Wrexham Central and Wrexham Exchange stations were published in the following year, but there was considerable opposition to the withdrawal of passenger services from the aptly-named station - which was indeed centrally placed in relation to the centre of the town. It was also pointed out that the line through Wrexham Central was still needed to convey tank traffic to and from Maelor Gas Plant, and for this reason the proposed closure would not necessarily produce significant savings.

Proposals for the closure of Wrexham Central and Exchange stations with effect from 4th May, 1970 were published, but the Minister of the Environment refused to sanction the proposed withdrawal, and Wrexham Central station therefore remained in operation. Conversely, at the other end of the Wrexham & Ellesmere route, Ellesmere had been closed to passenger traffic on 18th January, 1965 and to freight with effect from 29th March.

Post-Closure Developments

Reverting briefly to the history of Marchwiel Ordnance Factory, it will be recalled that Marchwiel Factory sidings were worked under the terms of a private siding agreement made on 12th August, 1941. This was formally terminated on 17th July, 1961, but the sidings at Marchwiel Factory had remained in use under a new agreement made between BR and the Wales & Monmouthshire Industrial Estates Company Ltd - the former government facilities at Marchwiel Factory having become the Wrexham Trading Estate.

Maelor Siding, at the southern end of the Marchwiel Factory site, continued to produce at least some rail traffic, steam engines being employed until 1967. Interestingly, the Wrexham area was by that time one of the last parts of the former Great Western system to be used by steam engines. The Great Central Shed at Wrexham Rhosddu was closed in January 1960, and its remaining locomotives were transferred to Wrexham Croes Newydd; the latter shed was itself closed to steam in March 1967, but BR Standard class '9F' 2-10-0s and ex-LMS 'Black Five' 4-6-0s worked from Birkenhead until the following November.

Bangor-on-Dee station after closure, looking south along the down platform towards Ellesmere. The goods shed can be seen in the distance. *S.C. Jenkins/Lens of Sutton Collection*

Ex-Great Western '57XX' class pannier tanks including Nos. 3749 and 9610 were still active in and around Wrexham in 1966, but these were gradually replaced by LMR types on local duties. Diesels had assumed full command of traffic on the Marchwiel line by 1967, by which time Croes Newydd had an allocation of four English Electric type '4' 1Co-Co1s (later class '40s') for work on oil tank trains to and from the trading estate; the engines concerned were Nos. D325, D339, D342 and D369.

More typical, perhaps, in the final twilight years of freight operation, were class '25' Bo-Bos such as Nos. 25166 and 25291, both of which appeared at various times on the Abenbury brick works trips.

Sadly, any hope that the remaining portion of the Wrexham & Ellesmere line would be retained as a specialist freight-carrying route were groundless, and the surviving services were slowly whittled away during the 1970s. The line was said to be out of use beyond Marchwiel by December 1971, and in May 1973 the railway was cut back to Abenbury Siding. Thereafter, the severely downgraded line eked out a precarious existence for a few more years, but the end finally came in May 1981, when remaining freight services were withdrawn.

In retrospect, the closure of what was left of the Wrexham & Ellesmere Railway was probably inevitable. The decline of traditional industries, coupled with the insidious growth of road transport presaged doom for local freight services up and down the country, but in the case of the Wrexham & Ellesmere line the situation was worsened by the precarious condition of the viaducts at various places along the line.

Jack Wilkinson considered that the poor condition of an underline bridge between Trench Halt and Elson Halt had hastened the end of passenger services back in 1962, while it is equally likely that the expense of maintaining the Dee bridge at Bangor mitigated against the continuance of freight traffic south of Pickhill Halt. In the next few years, as less and less maintenance was carried out on the freight-only line, the remaining bridges and viaducts began to deteriorate until such a point that major repairs would have become necessary.

Despite these problems, there was an attempt to keep the remaining portion of the line in being on the assumption that it might one day be needed - in effect the route could be 'moth-balled' until it was needed for goods or perhaps even passenger traffic. In the latter context, it was pointed out that the existing diesel service on the former Wrexham, Mold & Connah's Quay line still ran into Wrexham Central station - from where it could easily be extended southeastwards to serve new residential developments along the route of the abondoned Wrexham & Ellesmere Railway.

Alun Jenkins, and other local councillors, argued that the largely elevated route through Wrexham had cost a lot of money to build, and once it was destroyed any possibility of restoring the railway would be lost forever. Regrettably, this argument carried little weight, and the line was subsequently dismantled. The overbridges, and some of the embankments, were ruthlessly demolished, though further east in the vicinity of Caia Road, some portions of the trackbed still remain.

The Railway Today

The closure and removal of the remaining freight-only line left Wrexham Central station in being as the one tangible link with the past. In the next few years, the station underwent severe rationalisation, and by the 1980s only one platform (the former platform 3) remained in use. Car parks and unsightly urban wasteland impinged on all sides, and the only passenger accommodation was a crude, open-fronted waiting shelter. The line ended abruptly on the western abutment of the dismantled Vicarage Road overbridge, the terminal buffer stop being sited within a few feet of the road.

Looking westwards from this scene of utter desolation, Bradley Road bridge extended from north to south across the site of the abandoned goods yard. Quite apart from the progressive removal of the railway infrastructure at Wrexham Central, there had also been much demolition of property around the semi-derelict station site - the most significant casualty being St Mark's Church, which had once dominated the entire site.

The former Great Central signal box at Wrexham Central was threatened with demolition in 1988, but it transpired that a GCR-type box was needed for use on the preserved Great Central Railway at Birstall, and the old Wrexham, Mold & Connah's Quay box was dismantled and transported to Leicestershire in October 1988. The frame was found to be a 28-lever example made by the Railway Signalling Company of Fazakerley, Liverpool around 1900.

There had, for several years been various plans for a comprehensive redevelopment of the entire site. It was suggested that the line could be cut back towards Wrexham Exchange, leaving more space for redevelopment, but there was considerable opposition to such a move, which would place the single platform at a slightly greater distance from the main shopping areas. On a more positive note, it was stipulated that if the station was re-sited there should be sufficient space for a second terminal platform to cater for future traffic growth.

These tentative plans came to fruition in the late 1990s. On 6th May, 1997 the Rail Regulator agreed that Wrexham Central station - which was by that time owned by Railtrack and operated by North Western Trains - could be closed. He stipulated that the closure would only take place after a replacement station had

A recent view of Ellesmere station building from the road. The building remains remarkably unchanged over the years. *S.C. Jenkins*

Wrexham station in 1998; the rationalised facilities were in marked contrast to the busy station of former years. The remains of the Ellesmere line are beyond the stop blocks. *S.C. Jenkins*

THE FINAL YEARS : 1948-1982

been built, while the latter station would have sufficient room for future extensions and enhancements. Accordingly, the new station was opened on 23rd November, 1998, allowing the old station to be closed.

The new terminus is an attractive, modern structure that provides a vastly-improved environment for rail-users. It is slightly further from the town centre than its predecessor, but still within easy walking distance of the main shopping and business areas. The old Wrexham Central site has now been completely re-developed, and very few traces now remain of the station once used by Wrexham & Ellesmere branch services.

At the other end of the Wrexham & Ellesmere line, Ellesmere station building has survived in private hands, and much of the formation between Hightown and Cambrian Junction can still be followed on foot or by car. The abandoned railway will probably last for centuries as a landscape feature - just as Roman roads, Saxon earthworks, Medieval field patterns and other relics of man's activities have survived as tangible reminders of ancient times.

On a more prosaic level, at least one of the steel-panelled BR-built auto-coaches used on the line has found a new lease of life on a preserved railway, although none of the engines employed regularly on the route have survived.

The impressive facade of the new Wrexham Central station seen shortly after opening. The local rail users group objected to the resiting of Wrexham Central because of the greater walking distance from the town centre to the new station. Their objections were overruled, however, and the proposals went ahead. The end result is a vastly improved environment for rail users compared to the rundown facilities which it replaced. For more information and images on the railways around Wrexham in recent times visit www.penmorfa.com
D. Sallery

The new station at Wrexham Central. Class '101' dmu No. 101682 of Longsight depot, Manchester forms a Bidston service on 6th September, 1999. These class '101' trains have finally been taken out of regular service on the line after many years of use. Because of the steep gradients between Wrexham and Bidston all dmus had to be powered twin sets. The single platform at the new station is able to accomodate a three-car unit.   *D. Sallery*

Addendum: The Unfinished WM&CQ Line at Kings Mill

Mention of abandoned earthworks in the landscape serves as a reminder that the unfinished works of the abortive WM&CQ Whitchurch extension can still be seen. It is believed that work on this scheme commenced in 1866, but was then halted during the economic crisis that followed the collapse of the Overend & Gurney bank in May 1866.

The half mile of line that had been completed before work finally ceased began near Hightown, at the side of a lane that was then called Brynycabanau. Running eastwards, the unfinished line ran through cuttings for quarter of a mile to Kings Mills Road, at which point an overbridge would have been required; continuing eastwards, the earthworks ran through further cuttings for 21 chains, and then approached the Clywedog valley on an embankment that extended eastwards for 22 chains before coming to an abrupt halt.

The trackless earthworks survived for many years, but much of the cutting, had been filled-in by the 1930s, and modern residential developments have now obscured much of the route. At the eastern end, however, the embankment has been landscaped as part of Mill Gardens and the Gwenfro River Walk.

It is conceivable that parts of the original 1860s route at Kings Mill were incorporated into the Wrexham & Ellesmere line when construction resumed in the 1890s, though the clay pits at Abenbury Brick Works make precise interpretation difficult. Moreover, the WM&CQ line would have followed a different route, with the result that the earlier line would have bridged the Clywedog River at an angle to the Wrexham & Ellesmere alignment. At its western end the WM&CQ line would have curved north-westwards beyond the Brynycabanau lane and crossed the GWR line to the north of the Union Workhouse, but this portion of the line was never commenced.

Appendix One

Chronology

1861	Formation of the Wrexham, Mold & Connah's Quay Railway (October).
1862	Incorporation of Wrexham, Mold & Connah's Quay Railway (7th August).
1863	Proposed WM&CQ extension from Wrexham to Whitchurch.
1864	Formation of the Cambrian Railways (by amalgamation).
	Wrexham, Mold & Connah's Quay Railway Extension Act (25th July).
	Opening of the Oswestry, Ellesmere & Whitchurch Railway (27th July).
1865	Wrexham, Mold & Connah's Quay Railway Farndon Extension Act (29th June).
1866	Wrexham, Mold & Connah's Quay Railway Whitchurch (Deviations) Act.
	Wrexham, Mold & Connah's Quay Railway main line opened (1st May).
	WM&CQ begins work on the proposed Wrexham to Whitchurch line.
1867	Failure of bankers Overend, Gurney & Co. creates economic crisis.
	Wrexham, Mold & Connah's Quay obtains extension of time.
1873	Formal abandonment of the proposed Whitchurch extension line (November).
1882	New route surveyed from Wrexham to Bettisfield, near Ellesmere.
	WM&CQ obtains Act for extension to Wrexham Central (18th August).
1884	Bill for proposed Denbighshire & Shropshire Union Railway (aborted).
1885	Incorporation of Wrexham & Ellesmere Railway (31st July).
1887	Opening of WM&CQ extension to Wrexham Central (1st November).
1888	Deaths of Benjamin Piercy and Henry Robertson (original W&E promoters).
	Wrexham & Ellesmere obtains extension of time (10th August).
1889	The Welsh Railways Through Traffic Act.
1890	Opening of Buckley Junction to Chester line (31st March).
	Wrexham & Ellesmere Railway obtains further extension of time (22nd May).
1891	Proposed joint scheme for construction of the Wrexham & Ellesmere line by the Cambrian, Great Western & Manchester, Sheffield & Lincolnshire companies (not proceeded with).
1892	Contract for construction let to Messrs Davies Brothers.
	Cutting of first sod (11th July).
1895	Wrexham & Ellesmere Railway obtains powers for loop at Ellesmere (May).
	First passenger train run from Wrexham to Ellesmere (2nd August).
	Board of Trade inspection (24th September).
	Opening of Wrexham & Ellesmere Railway (2nd November).
1904	Private siding agreement signed for use of Five Fords Siding (January).
1905	WM&CQ Railway absorbed by Great Central (1st January).
1913	Opening of Sesswick Halt (October).
1914	Private siding agreement for use of Kings Mill Siding (24th July).
	Start of World War I (4th August).
	Opening of Trench Halt (December).
1918	End of World War I (11th November).
1922	Wrexham & Ellesmere Railway absorbed by GWR (1st July).
1923	Opening of Hightown Halt (9th July).
1930	Closure of Ellesmere Junction signal box.
1932	Opening of Cloy Halt (30th June).
1937	Opening of Elson Halt (8th February).
1938	Opening of Pickhill Halt (30th May).
	Private siding agreement for use of Trench Siding (21st April).
1939	Start of World War II (3rd September).

THE WREXHAM & ELLESMERE RAILWAY

1939   Railways taken into government control (from 1st September).
Restricted wartime timetable introduced (25th September).
1940   Fall of France (May-June).
Passenger service suspended between Wrexham & Ellesmere (8th June).
1941   Private siding agreement for use of Marchwiel Factory Sidings (August).
Closure of Trench Siding.
1945   End of war in Europe (7th May).
End of war with Japan (14th August).
1946   Reinstatement of passenger services (6th May).
1947   Private siding agreement for use of Hightown Siding (20th December).
1948   Nationalisation of British railway system (1st January).
1955   Private siding agreement for Five Fords Siding terminated (31st December).
1961   New private siding agreement for Marchwiel Factory Siding.
1961   Proposal for closure of Wrexham & Ellesmere line.
1962   Withdrawal of passenger services between Wrexham and Ellesmere (exclusive) and complete closure south of Pickhill Halt (8th September).
1963   Publication of Beeching Plan for re-organisation of BR (March).
Demolition of line between Pickhill and Ellesmere.
1965   Proposed closure of Wrexham, Mold & Connah's Quay line (November).
1968   Wrexham, Mold & Connah's Quay line reprieved.
1970   New proposal for closure of Wrexham Central station (not sanctioned).
1973   Wrexham & Ellesmere line cut back to Abenbury Siding.
1981   Wrexham & Ellesmere Railway closed in its entirety south of Wrexham.
1988   Wrexham Central signal box moved to Great Central Railway (October).
1997   Resiting of Wrexham Central station.
1998   Opening of replacement station to west of the original.

Wrexham Central on 25th August, 1962, with dmus for Bidston or Chester Northgate in the bay platform. The auto train service to Ellesmere is at the far end of the through platform.

Appendix Two

Facilities at Halts and Stations

Although full details of each station have been given in Chapters Four and Five, it may be worth describing the infrastructure of the Wrexham & Ellesmere branch in a more formalised way, and the following section has therefore been included in the hope that it may be of use for modellers (and others) seeking factual information about each station and halt.

Ellesmere

Up and down platforms
1,158 ft crossing loop with intermediate crossover road
Refuge siding on up side with capacity for 38-wagon freight trains
Brick-built station building on down side and brick/timber shelter up side
Station and Junction signal boxes (the latter closed in 1930)
Pedestrian footbridge
'Mushroom' type water tank on up platform
Brick goods shed
Cattle pens, loading dock and six-ton fixed hand crane
Weigh-house, lamp hut and permanent way huts, etc.

Elson Halt

Earth & timber passenger platform, on down side (length 75 ft)
Waiting shelter
Elson Siding (21 chains south of the halt)

Trench Halt

Earth and timber platform on up side (45 ft)
Waiting shelter
Trench Siding (6 chains to north of halt)

Overton-on-Dee

Up and down platforms
675 ft crossing loop
Timber building on down platform and timber waiting shelter on up side
Signal box
Goods shed, cattle pens, loading dock and six-ton fixed hand crane
Weigh-house, coal wharves, etc.

Cloy Halt

Earth and timber platform on down side (length 75 ft)
Great Western-type arc-roofed corrugated iron shelter

142 THE WREXHAM & ELLESMERE RAILWAY

Bangor-on-Dee

Up and down platforms
804 ft crossing loop
Timber buildings on down platform and timber waiting shelter on up side
Signal box
Goods shed, cattle pens and loading dock
Weigh-house, coal wharves and permanent way sheds, etc.

Pickhill Halt

Wooden passenger platform on down side (length 100 ft)
Passenger waiting shelter
Private siding connection to Cadbury's Creamery

Sesswick Halt

Earth and concrete-edged platform on down side (length 240 ft)
Wooden waiting shelter

Marchwiel

Up and down platforms
771 ft crossing loop with intermediate crossover
Timber building on down side and timber waiting shelter on up platform
Signal box
Cattle pens, loading docks, etc.
Weigh-house and coal wharves
Five Fords private siding (30 chains to south)

Hightown Halt

Earth and timber platform on down side (length 98 ft)
Waiting shelter
Private siding (19 chains to south of halt)

Wrexham Caia Goods Depot

Goods shed
Cattle pens, loading docks and $1\frac{1}{2}$ ton fixed hand crane.

Wrexham Central

Up and down through platforms and three dead-end bays
Timber and corrugated iron station buildings
Brick goods shed
Two signal boxes
Cattle pens, coal wharves, loading docks and 5 ton fixed yard crane
Water column (No. 3 platform only)
50 ft locomotive turntable
Private siding connection to Cobden's flour mill

A Guide to Further Study

Published material on the Wrexham & Ellesmere Railway is virtually non-existent, but the following select bibliography may be of interest to modellers or local historians seeking further information.

Auden, John Ernest, *The Little Guide to Shropshire* (1912).
Bolger, Paul, *BR Steam Motive Power Depots: ER* (1982).
Boyd, James C., *The Wrexham, Mold & Connah's Quay Railway* (1991).
Bradshaw's Railway Guides, passim.
Bradshaw's Railway Shareholders Guide, passim.
British Railways, *Public & Working Timetables.*
British Railways, *Permanent Way Alterations, Signalling Instructions, Etc.*
Copsey, John, 48XX Auto Engines, *Great Western Railway Journal* Nos. 22 & 23, 1997.
Copsey, John, '2251' Class Mixed Traffic 0-6-0s, *Great Western Railway Journal*, No. 24, 1997.
Cummings, John, *Railway Motor Buses & Bus Services* (1980).
Dow, George, *Great Central Railway*, 2 vols, *passim.*
Draper, K.G., Ellesmere & the Wrexham Branch, *Railway Modeller*, January 1987.
Dunn, L.M., *The Wrexham, Mold & Connah's Quay Railway.*
Freezer, Cyril J., Locomotives of the GWR: Push-pull Panniers, *Railway Modeller*, September 1969.
Freezer, Cyril J., Locomotives of the GWR: 14XX Class 0-4-2T, *Railway Modeller*, October 1967,
Freezer, Cyril J., Locomotives of the GWR: The Ubiquitous Pannier, *Railway Modeller*, June 1967.
Gourvish, T.R., *British Railways 1948- 73: A Business History* (1986).
Great Western Railway, *Traffic Dealt with at Stations & Goods Depots*, (PRO RAIL 253/45),
Great Western Railway, *Towns, Villages, Outlying Works etc* (1938).
Great Western Railway, *Working & Public Timetables, passim.*
Great Western Railway, *Station Accounts Instruction Book* (1929).
Great Western Railway Magazine, The, passim.
Holcroft, H., *An Outline of Great Western Locomotive Practice 1837-1947* (1947).
Hughes, Gervase, British Express Train Services in 1898, *The Railway Magazine*, April 1961.
Jenkins, S.C. & Strange, J.M., The Gobowen to Oswestry Branch, *Great Western Railway Journal*, No.22 1997.
Jenkins, Stanley C., The Wrexham, Mold & Connah's Quay Railway, *Steam Days* No. 165, May 2003.
Jones, P.T., *The Welsh Marches* (no date).
Kidner, R.W., *The Mid-Wales Railway* (1990).
Kidner, R.W., *The Cambrian Railways* (1992).
Lloyd, Michael, Cambrian Railways 2-4-0T, *Railway Modeller*, March 1965.
Lloyd, Michael, GWR (ex-Cambrian Railways) 0-6-0, *Railway Modeller*, May 1967.
Locomotive Magazine, The, September 1913-August 1914.
Lyons, Eric, *An Historical Survey of Great Western Engine Sheds* (1972).
MacDermot, E.T., *History of the Great Western Railway* Vols. I & II (1927).
Minnis J., & Lloyd, M., A Cambrian Collection, *British Railway Journal* No. 7, Spring 1985.
Proceedings of the Institute of Civil Engineers, passim.
Railway Clearing House, *Handbook of Stations* (various editions).
Railway Times, The, passim.
Rear, Bill, Railways of Wrexham, *Steam Days* No. 123, November 1999.
Shropshire Magazine, The, passim.
Smith, Martin, An Anonymous Class - The GWR 81XX Class 2-6-2Ts, *British Railways Illustrated*, July 1999.
Storey, Alfred T., *The Little Guide to North Wales* (1907).
Tolson, John M., The Wrexham & Ellesmere Line, *Railway World*, June 1965.
Tolson, John M., Great Central on the Welsh Border, *The Railway Magazine*, January-February 1972.
Wrexham Advertiser, The, 2nd November 1895 *et passim.*
Wrexham Argus, The, February 1895, August 1865 *et passim.*

Index

Abenbury Brick Works 36, 59, 102-103, 117, 134
Accidents 67, 69
Ambulance trains, WWII, 63, 64
Aslett, A.H. (engineer), 18, 29, 31, 33, 35, 79

Bangor-on-Dee station, 34, 35, 49, 55, 56, 57, 59, 85-89, 117, 128, 134, 142
Beeching Plan, The, 131, 140
Brymbo Steel Works, 107

Cadbury's Creamery Siding (Pickhill) 55, 57, 59, 91, 92, 93, 117, 124, 125, 131, 142
Cambrian Railways, formation of, 11
Cheshire Lines Committee, 13, 15, 39, 47
Closures, 127, 131, 133, 140
Cloy Halt, 54, 56, 57, 59, 83, 84, 117, 132, 139, 141
Clywedog Viaduct, see Kings Mill Viaduct
Coal merchants, 58, 59, 69

Davies, Howel & Llewelyn (contractors) 18, 21, 23, 30, 31, 35, 36, 103
Davis, William, 14, 17
Dee viaduct, 7, 34, 35, 36, 89, 90, 117, 123, 134

Ellesmere Old Loop Siding, 51, 59, 61, 62, 72-73, 117
Ellesmere station, 35, 46, 51, 55, 56, 59, 65-73, 117, 118, 129, 136, 141
Elson Halt, 54, 56, 59, 62, 74-75, 117, 139, 141
Elson Siding, 56, 57, 59, 62, 75-76, 117, 125, 139, 140, 141

Five Fords Farm Siding, 57, 59, 62, 101, 117, 139
Forge Mill viaduct, 2, 25, 101, 117
Freight traffic, 47, 55, 56, 57, 59, 60, 61, 63, 69, 73, 75, 77, 83, 85, 87, 91, 93, 95, 101, 103, 105, 107, 121, 124, 130, 131, 134

Garibaldi, Guissepe, 17

Heber, Bishop R., 29
Hightown Halt, 45, 55, 59, 105, 106, 117, 139, 142
Hightown Siding, 59, 105, 117

Industrial locomotives, 22-23, 24, 36, 95, 97

Jellicoe Specials, 47

Kenyon, George (W&E Chairman), 19, 20, 21, 35
Kings Mill Siding, 57, 59, 102, 103, 105, 117
Kings Mill Viaduct, 2, 7, 25, 35, 102, 104, 105, 117, 139

Liveries, 37, 39, 119
Locomotives, 33, 37-41, 42 50, 51, 52, 64, 119-120, 133, 134

Manchester, Sheffield & Lincolnshire Railway 13, 14, 15, 16, 19, 43
Marchwiel Factory, 61, 93, 95, 97, 117, 131, 133

Marchwiel station, 32, 35, 49, 55, 56, 59, 95-101, 117, 128, 142
Marples, Ernest, 125

North Wales Mineral Railway, 9

Oswestry 9, 35, 54 *et passim*
Oswestry & Newtown Railway, 9, 10, 11
Oswestry, Ellesmere & Whitchurch Railway 9, 10, 11, 12
Oughtibridge Silica Firebrick Co., 103
Overend, Gurney & Co., 13, 139
Overton-on-Dee station, 35, 49, 55, 56, 59, 63, 64, 78-83, 84, 117, 121, 126, 127, 129, 132, 141
Owen, George (engineer), 18, 20, 29, 31, 33, 35, 89

Pickhill Halt, 54, 56, 59, 91-93, 117, 126, 139, 142
Piercy, Benjamin (promoter), 14, 17, 21, 139
Plas-yn-Grove viaduct, 123
Pollitt William, 19, 29, 35

Rhosddu locomotive shed, 52, 53, 115, 117, 133
Road feeder services, 54-57, 69, 73, 85
Robertson, Henry (promoter), 14, 17, 139
Rolling stock, 39, 58, 59, 121
Rubery Owen Ltd, 105

Sesswick Halt, 47, 56, 59, 62, 93-94, 117, 139, 142
Shrewsbury & Chester Railway, 9
Standing Conference of Welsh Railways, 15

Tickets (Illustrated) 49, 122
Town Hill viaduct, 35, 107, 112, 117
Train services, 43, 47, 53-54, 60, 61, 63, 121, 124
Trench Halt, 47, 56, 59, 76-77, 117, 139, 141
Trench Siding, 59, 77, 117, 141

Watkin, Sir Edward, 13,19
Welsh Railways Through Traffic Act 1889, 15, 139
Willow Road Viaduct, 2, 7, 35, 107, 117
Wirral Railway, 15
World War I, 47, 49, 139
World War II, 60-64, 75, 77, 83, 93, 101, 105, 121, 140
Wrexham & District Electric Tramways, 45, 115
Wrexham & Ellesmere Railway, construction of, 19-29
Wrexham & Ellesmere Railway, formation of 14-17
Wrexham & Ellesmere Railway, opening of, 29-35
Wrexham Brick & Tile Co., 47, 103
Wrexham Caia Goods Depot, 36, 54, 59, 60, 107, 108, 115, 142
Wrexham Central station, 20, 32, 42, 56, 59, 107-117, 135-138, 139, 140, 142
Wrexham Exchange station, 20, 115
Wrexham, Mold & Connah's Quay Railway, 10, 11, 13, 14, 15, 16, 17, 19, 20, 37, 53, 87, 105, 109, 113, 124, 131, 139, 140 *et passim*

144